Atlas
of Indians
of North America

Written and Illustrated by

Gilbert Legay

FOREST HOUSE ®

School & Library Edition

CONTENTS

"WHAT A ROAD WE'VE TRAVELED, YOU AND I!"

CROW

"**W**here are the Pequot today? Where are the Narragansett, the Mohawk, the Pokanoket, and all the other tribes that once were so powerful. They vanished before the greed and oppression of the white man like snow in the summer sun."

This dramatic cry of the great Shawnee chief Tecumseh came at the moment when the United States, still a young nation in the early nineteenth century, began its conquest of the West. Tecumseh could not have known that many of the other Indian nations or tribes would survive, some would increase in population, and many would begin new economic endeavors into the twentieth century and beyond.

Native America is often presented through the distorted prism of Western movies, cartoons, or popular novels—media sometimes not inclined to go beyond the usual stereotypes. Gilbert Legay's work avoids stereotypes in presenting the world of Native America with all its rich diversity and complexity. The author has adopted an approach developed by American anthropologists of representing Indian Nations in their particular environments or cultural areas. This atlas depicts tribes or nations in a geographical framework that reflects the unique relationship between Indian people and their natural environment.

The illustrations are based upon significant ethnographic documentation. They describe Native American life in its splendor, an interpretation history often brushes aside without a trace. The text and illustrations inspire the reader to consider the fate of Native Americans and their significant contributions to contemporary life. These contributions far outweigh the small population on the North American continent of only about three million. Agriculture, religion, arts, and tribal governments are but a few of the elements of Native culture that have influenced life in countries throughout the Western Hemisphere.

In the film *Dances with Wolves*, the Sioux shaman, Kicking Bird, pleased to be able to talk with Lieutenant John Dunbar, who has become a Sioux, and proud of their friendship, tells him in confidence, "What a road we've traveled, you and I!" The difficulties people have in understanding one another and other cultures, and in listening to one another, are reflected in these few words. This book is a guide to help show you the way. ▲

Philippe Jacquin

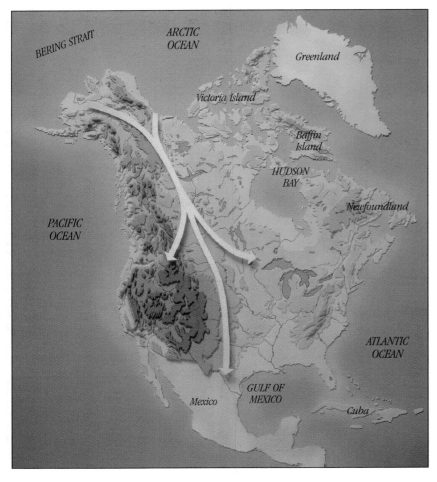

Hunters came from Siberia and inhabited the American continent. Taking advantage of favorable conditions created by glacial changes, they crossed over on a bridge of ice the passage that is known today as the Bering Strait. Two important migration eras appear to be the time between 36,000 and 32,000 years ago and from 26,000 to 12,000 years ago. Although these dates are approximate, a hypothesis some scholars have not ruled out is that new research may provide evidence of ancient populations that existed even earlier.

During historical times they referred to themselves as:

NAVAJO—"DI-NEH," THE PEOPLE

SHOSHONE—"SOSONEES," SNAKE PEOPLE

UTE—"NU-CI," INDIAN PEOPLE

TLINGIT—"LI-NGIT," HUMAN BEINGS

HAIDA—"HA-TE," THE PEOPLE

CHIPEWYAN—"CI-PWAYA-N," THOSE WITH POINTED SKINS OR HIDES

TSIMSHIAN—"'CMSYAN," INSIDE THE SKEENE RIVER

INUIT—"INUIT," PERSON, PEOPLE

FOREWORD

They lived in many different environments, worshipping elements of nature such as the sun and thunder.

They sought harmony with nature, respecting both flora and fauna.

They honored the earth and were often defeated by those who wanted to own it.

They were brave, yet history often portrayed a distorted view. "Redskins" referred to their brown skin. The term "Indians" linked them to a land that was not their own and that honored a navigator who was not the first to discover it.

They were worthy of respect but were treated like savages by invaders who brought with them wars, disease, violence, and greed.

History provides only a few voices raised in protest, in fairness, and with justice. Could a different course have been followed?

Swedish colonists established good relations with Native American neighbors. William Penn's Quakers also came in peace, aware that they were trespassing on original Native territories.

Some pioneers and woodsmen of New France had friendly relations with Native Americans, sharing their lives and marrying their daughters.

These were some of the all too few exceptions.

The purpose of this book is to introduce the reader to Native American life, depicted in the ten environmental areas most commonly described by scientists—ethnographers and archaeologists. Included in each region are often the largest and best known Native groups, with each represented according to the origin or etymology of their name, linguistic family, geographic location, cultural features, key facts of their history, and present status of their tribe. By drawing upon the work of nineteenth- and twentieth-century painters, designers, and photographers' testimonies, the rendered illustrations give a visual history of the people, while presenting vital aspects of their natural surroundings. Cultural areas are, to a great extent, approximate, as the boundaries between peoples were vague and changed over time. Also, as a result of space limitations, the information presented here is an incomplete story. Cultural traits are mentioned only briefly and these include languages, beliefs, tribal or family organization, weaponry, hunting and fishing techniques, the arts, and some of the roles of women. The reader will find more thorough and complete information in further research focusing on in-depth studies of the history and ethnology of Native American life. ▲

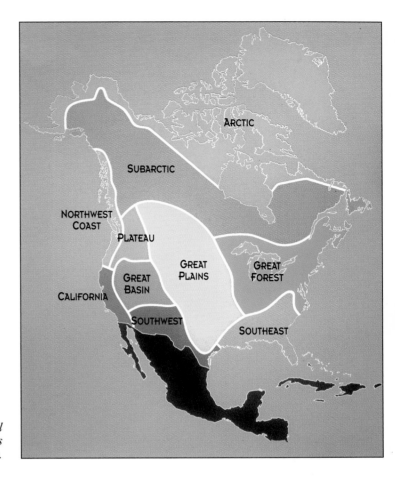

The North American continent has been divided into ten environmental areas, each corresponding to an area in which the Native inhabitants shared similar ways of life.

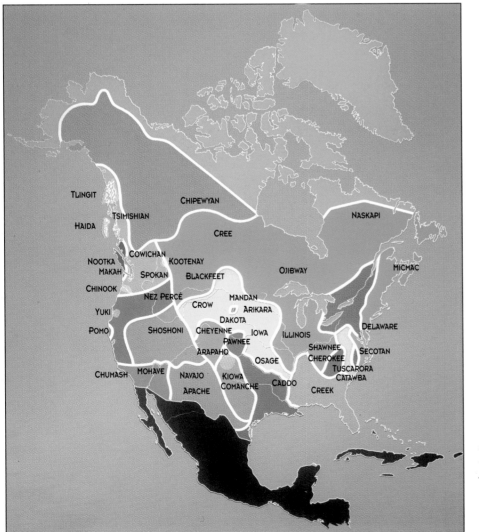

ESKIMO-ALEUT

ATHAPASKAN

ALGONQUIAN

IROQUOIAN

SIOUAN

MUSKOGEAN

CADDOAN

SHOSHONEAN

HOKAN

SHAHAPTIAN-PENUTIAN

SALISHAN

WAKASHAN

This map shows the general areas of the twelve largest Native American linguistic families that have been identified in North America. Languages were subdivided under a larger language family, each having numerous derivatives, and each smaller tribal unit defining itself over time by its own linguistic identity. It is estimated that more than 2,000 languages were spoken when Europeans first arrived, but only about 200 of them have been identified. Some tribal names are mentioned as a reference.

THE SOUTHEAST

As the European age of discovery in North America came to an end, the age of exploration and conquest began. Arriving first in the West Indies, Spanish armies set out to conquer and convert the New World to Christianity. Within a few decades, the Gulf of Mexico became a Spanish sea and expeditions set forth to the west and to the south. Belief in the seeming narrowness of the new continent was prevalent and Balboa's voyage to the Pacific Ocean in 1513 reinforced the idea. The search for the hypothetical passage to India, the lure of riches, and the taste for conquest heightened the aspirations of the Spaniards.

The North seemed less promising for riches and glory. At first, there were only small expeditions such as the one launched by Ponce de León. Landing on the continent on March 27, 1513, he entered a luxuriant wilderness. But it was not the attraction of unknown territory that compelled the old soldier. Nor was he risking his life for the glory of the King of Spain. Having recently married a young and beautiful wife, Ponce de León's goal was to discover the legendary source of eternal youth recounted in sailors' legends. He was hoping to recapture his youthful passion through the reputed powers of the spiritual water.

During the first voyage, the Spaniards killed some members of the Calusa tribes. By the end of the second journey, some eight years later, Native Americans killed almost the entire expedition in revenge. Ponce de León was struck by an arrow and died on his return to Cuba. He had not found the fountain of youth, and many Native people would, henceforth, fight against the Spanish incursion. In increasingly greater numbers thereafter, Vasquez de Ayllon, Panfilo de Narvaez, and Hernando de Soto landed in Florida and tried to establish a route through the jungle. All three lost their lives in the attempts. The Spanish temporarily abandoned plans to conquer Florida but in the second half of the sixteenth century, when the French and the English attempted to establish colonies there, the Spanish reacted in order to protect a region they considered within their sphere of political influence. Spain, France, and England sometimes antagonized each other through Native American intermediaries whom each major power had won to its side. In less than two centuries, incessant wars and epidemics contributed to the disappearance of many Native groups on the Atlantic.

The Southeast region stretches from the Atlantic Coast to the Mississippi Valley, and from Tennessee to the Gulf of Mexico. Before the Europeans arrived, the American Indian people of the region lived close to nature, in a mild, humid climate. It is possible more than one million people inhabited the region at the beginning of the sixteenth century. ▲

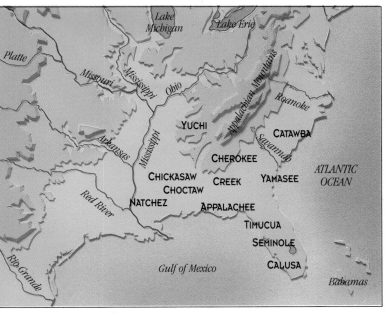

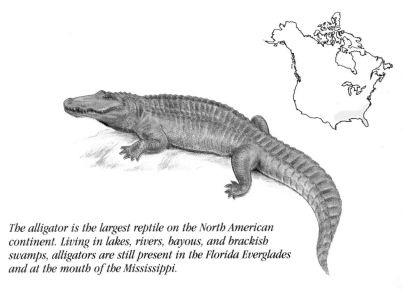

The alligator is the largest reptile on the North American continent. Living in lakes, rivers, bayous, and brackish swamps, alligators are still present in the Florida Everglades and at the mouth of the Mississippi.

Based on Fontaneda's description, around 1650.

CALUSA

♦ According to Hernando Fontaneda, who was a prisoner of the Calusa for several years, their name was translated as "the wild people," however, this translation may have been a distortion by the Spanish King Charles V.

♦ Language: Muskogean.

♦ They lived in southern Florida.

♦ Archeological excavations indicate that their ancestors inhabited the region about 1400 B.C. Skillful woodcarvers, the Calusa were also farmers and fishermen. They traded with Cuba and possibly the Acetin. Human sacrifices were a part of their rituals.

♦ Their fleet of eighty boats drove Ponce de León away in 1513; however, the Spanish colonized Florida by the end of the century.

♦ The Calusa population was estimated at 3,000 in 1650. A century later, a few survivors joined their neighbors, the Seminole, while others fled to Cuba.

A few minor disputes broke out among the Native American tribes, for the joy of combat as much as for the protection of their hunting grounds. The decision to start a war was discussed at length between the tribal elders and the chief. If they decided to fight, a war chief, whose first task was to boost the morale of the men, was chosen. Next came the ritual preparations, which could last several days and were an indispensable physical and mental conditioning for battle. The men could no longer have any contact with women. They had to observe a complete fast and to take plant-based emetics. This quest for purity was accompanied by dances and stories relating the exploits of their ancestors. These preparations ended with a feast that included the meat from animals noted for their courage (stags) or loyalty (dogs). As an ultimate precaution, they consulted soothsayers. If the signs were unfavorable, the enterprise was halted; if favorable, the warriors departed, some painted in red and black—the colors of war and death. The mission was brief: kill, scalp, take prisoners, "sign" the raid, and come home in triumph. The return of the victorious warriors ignited celebrations lasting for several days. At their conclusion, the fate of the prisoners was decided—either adoption, slavery, or death.

Palisades surrounded the villages and a type of watchtower was often erected to guard against enemy raids. Each village was organized around the centers of activity—the council house, which was the gathering place of social and political activity, and an open area where young men practiced hunting techniques and where they played a sport known as lacrosse, which was a popular activity throughout the Southeast. Game sports were often ways to practice war and hunting skills.

There were many similarities in Southeast cultures and their basic ways of life. As skilled farmers who settled in a mild climate, they met the needs of their community (growing corn, squash, and sunflowers) without difficulty. Game was plentiful and the Native Americans were skilled hunters. According to the description by Jacques Le Moyne, a French draftsman and cartographer who lived in Florida around 1565, the hunters dressed in animal skins to approach their favorite animal, the deer, or to snare an alligator by driving a long, blunt spear down its throat. For small game or birds, the Cherokee used a blowpipe capable of projecting poisonous darts more than sixty feet (20 m). Native Americans had detailed knowledge of the medicinal properties of plants. The Cherokee and the Chickasaw used the stupefying effects of the chemical saponin to catch, effortlessly, nets full of fish. ▲

A plant of the sapindaceous family, the soapberry grows in the subtropical areas of the United States. The plant comes in a dozen or so species and contains saponin. Used as a natural cleanser, this foaming substance also paralyzes fish that are fond of the soapberry seeds. Native hunters used it successfully in catching fish in ponds and lakes.

*Turkeys (*Meleagis gallopavo*) roamed freely throughout the Southeast and were an important source of food for Native Americans all along the eastern forested areas. Some tribes, however, considered them cowardly and stupid, and refused to eat their flesh for fear of inheriting these faults.*

TIMUCUA

♦ Known also by the name of *utina* (chief), Timucua probably meant "sovereign" or "master."

♦ Language: Muskogean.

♦ They lived in northwestern Florida.

♦ Farmers, hunters, and fishermen, the Timucua lived in roundhouses grouped together in fortified villages. Very skillful merchants, they traded with Cuba.

♦ They were encountered by Ponce de León in 1513, Narvaez in 1528, de Soto in 1539, and Ribault in 1562. The Spanish supplanted the French and converted the Timucua before the latter, aided by the English, were decimated by the Creek, the Yuchi, and the Catawba.

♦ There were 13,000 around 1650. A century later, the Timucua had probably merged with other groups, becoming fewer in number.

APALACHEE

♦ From the Choctaw *apalachi*, "people of the other side" (of the Alabama River).

♦ Language: Muskogean.

♦ They lived in northeastern Florida.

♦ They arrived around the 14th century from west of the Mississippi, bringing the tradition of building temples on mounds. Formidable warriors, they were also hunters, fishermen, and farmers. They traded with the Timucua.

♦ Converted to Christianity by Spanish missionaries (17th century), the Apalachee were victims of English colonists and Creek (1703). Survivors supported the Yamassee Revolt (1715).

♦ By the beginning of the 19th century, many of the Apalachee tribe had either joined other tribes or disappeared.

In the style of John White, around 1650.

Based on a sixteenth-century etching.

Based on a seventeenth-century etching.

NATCHEZ

♦ The etymology is uncertain. Their name may translate to "warriors of the great cliff or high bluff."

♦ Language: Muskogean.

♦ They lived on the banks of the Mississippi.

♦ In addition to weaving, the Natchez had a well-developed social and ritual organization, centering around a chieftainship devoted to the sun. Their social organization followed a strict hierarchy.

♦ Once the largest Native group of the region, they were practically decimated during their revolt against the French in 1729–1730. Some survivors scattered among the neighboring tribes, such as the Chickasaw, while others were sent to Santo Domingo.

♦ Their population was estimated at 4,500 in 1650.

Based on a seventeenth-century etching.

Men's and women's roles were usually clearly defined in most Native American cultures. Men were often the hunters and fishermen. They usually cleared the soil for planting, built houses and palisades, and made weapons and canoes, while women planted, harvested, cooked, made pottery, wove baskets, tanned skins, and sewed clothing.

Because the family was the basic unit of Native American society, the marriage ceremony was an important event that could not be completed without a customary series of steps. For some of the Indian groups living in the Mississippi area, one of the young man's aunts had the responsibility of informing the young woman of the proposal.

On a specific day, the young woman would place a bowl of hominy in front of her house. The young man would ask for permission to eat this corn dish. If the young woman agreed, it was a sign that the proposal was accepted. The family of the husband-to-be would then prepare gifts, and the young couple could live together as man and wife under a new roof. After a year, if they were still living together, the marriage was considered official.

Other customs were important parts of the lives of the people from the Southeast. Some tribes practiced bigamy, but it usually involved a man marrying the sister of his first wife, which was considered a pledge of harmonious relations within the family. A widow waited a lengthy period of time (up to four years) before marrying again, unless she married a close relative of her deceased husband. Menstruation and pregnancies were accompanied by constraints and taboos. With the exception of the Natchez and the Timucua, whose monarchical societies depended on an inherited transmission of power, most of the Southeast groups maintained "democratic" principles, based on a matriarchal system. Chiefs were chosen for their guidance and wisdom. Some of the time they were also considered shaman and conducted religious ceremonies, but their political power was limited to guiding the debates of the council and assuming the role of chief conciliator. ▲

CREEK

♦ Their name comes from the English *creek*, for they lived on the borders of the Ochulgee River, which the Europeans called Ochese Creek. They called themselves *muskoke*, from the name of the dominant tribe.

♦ Language: Muskogean.

♦ They inhabited present-day Georgia and Alabama.

♦ A confederation of tribes gathered around the Muskoke. The Creek were excellent farmers, raising corn, squash, and sunflowers. They occasionally hunted and fished. Their villages were often fortified.

♦ Fighting beside the Yamassee during their revolt in 1715, they opposed the Cherokee for regional domination in 1753 and allied themselves with the English against the French and the Spanish. This did not prevent British colonists from invading their land. After American independence, the Creek led the Red Sticks Revolt in 1812–1814, which they lost. In 1836, they were forced into exile in Oklahoma.

♦ There were about 20,000 Creek at the beginning of the eighteenth century. Today, they have numerous descendants (12,000–40,000), who live mainly on reservations in Oklahoma.

Creek village.

Based on a seventeenth-century etching.

CHICKASAW

♦ The origin of their name is unknown.

♦ Language: Algonquian.

♦ They lived just north of present-day Mississippi.

♦ They were formidable warriors. The men hunted, fished, and built homes. The women worked in the fields.

♦ Allies of the English, the Chickasaw's role in the South was similar to that of the Iroquois in the North. Protective of their lands, they struggled against the Shawnee in 1715 and 1745, the Iroquois in 1732, the French in 1736, the Cherokee in 1768, and the Creek in 1795. They migrated to Oklahoma in 1822, where they obtained their own territory in 1855.

♦ Around 5,000 descendants remain in the middle of the twentieth century.

In the style of George Catlin, 1834.

CHOCTAW

♦ The meaning of their name is unclear. Perhaps from the Spanish *chato*, meaning "flat" or "to flatten," describing the skulls of children. They believed the flat skull gave piercing vision.) For this reason, the French called them "Flatheads."

♦ Language: Muskogean.

♦ They lived in southern Mississippi and Alabama.

♦ The Choctaw were less warlike than their neighbors and enemies, the Chickasaw. Dedicated agriculturists, they raised corn, sweet potatoes, and sunflowers. They also hunted, using bows and arrows and blowpipes.

♦ After the encounter with de Soto's expedition, 150 years passed without contact with Europeans. Allied with France, they were forced to migrate west of the Mississippi in 1780 after the French were defeated. In 1830, they turned over their land to the American government and were removed to Oklahoma.

♦ Around 20,000 lived in 115 villages at the beginning of the eighteenth century. According to the 1985 tribal census in Oklahoma and Mississippi, they numbered about 25,000.

CHEROKEE

♦ The etymology is uncertain. It is possibly a corruption of the word *Tsalagi*, "grotto people," the name they called themselves, or derived from the Creek *Tisolki*, "people of another language."

♦ Language: Iroquoian.

♦ They settled at the southern end of the Appalachians in present-day Carolinas, Georgia, and Tennessee.

♦ Farmers and hunters, the Cherokee were organized into seven clans of complex structures. Their sixty or so villages were grouped around the principal city, Echota.

♦ When de Soto encountered them in 1540, they were involved in all the bloody struggles of the region. When the colonists forced them to retreat, the Cherokee took part in the Little Turtle Revolt and in the Native American victory at Wabash in 1781. They tried to organize a nation modeled after the White nations. They invented a writing system, and published a weekly newspaper, the *Cherokee Phoenix*. But the advance of the colonists and the discovery of gold on their territory in 1826 precipitated their exile to Oklahoma, a journey that caused many to lose their lives on the infamous "Trail of Tears." They divided their allegiance during the Civil War, some helping the North, others the South.

♦ Estimated at 25,000 in 1650, their population was close to 50,000 in 1982. A great number of them live in Oklahoma, but more and more are returning to their ancestral homes in Tennessee and North Carolina.

Based on a 1762 etching.

PEOPLE OF THE SUN

YUCHI

♦ "People of another language," their Indian name *tsoya'ha* meant "children of the sun."

♦ Language: Siouan.

♦ They lived in east Tennessee and Georgia.

♦ Living in a region of small mountains, the Yuchi were independent and fierce warriors.

♦ In 1567, the Spanish inflicted heavy losses on them. Pressured by colonists, they migrated toward Creek territory in 1729, some following into Oklahoma, others joining the Seminole.

♦ Their population was estimated at 5,000 in the sixteenth century. The 1949 tribal census numbered their descendants at 1,216, half of whom were of mixed ancestry.

The coral snake (micrurus fulvius) *can measure as long as three feet (1.2 m). This venomous species inhabits both rocky and humid areas of heavy vegetation.*

CATAWBA

♦ Possible etymology from the Choctaw *katapa*, "divided" or "separated," or from the Yuchi *kotaba*, "robust men." Also known under the name of *issa* or *essa*, "river."

♦ Language: Siouan.

♦ They lived in the valley of the Wateree River in the two Carolinas.

♦ They were farmers, described in early literature as courageous and hospitable.

♦ They were part of a confederation of fifteen tribes. Enemies of the Cherokee, they were loyal to the English except in 1715, at the time of the Yamassee Revolt, then to the Americans.

♦ Severely afflicted by wars and smallpox, the Catawba numbered only a few hundred in 1775. In exile, some merged and intermarried the Cherokee. In 1944, the tribe in South Carolina numbered 300 and the last full-blooded Catawba reportedly died in 1962.

In the style of George Catlin, 1838.

Based on an eighteenth-century etching.

Well adapted to the environment, many Native Americans living in the Southeast divided the universe into different strata. Some believed in an upper world and underworld, and some in a third, middle level, where life was believed to be balanced.

Animals were often classified as winged, four-legged, and those that had direct contact with the earth, such as snakes, lizards, fish, and insects. Some animals were regarded with fear, such as bats, flying squirrels, frogs, turtles, owls, cougars, and snakes. Bears were considered special, for they were able to walk either on all fours or on two legs, like a man. Plant life was often classified according to whether the foliage was deciduous or evergreen.

For the Catawba, the real world was simple and logically constructed. They believed it could be compared to an island floating on water, suspended from heaven in the four cardinal directions. This vision was changed when the Spaniards arrived, followed by others who brought devastation, disease, and death to the Indian communities. ▲

The diamondback rattlesnake (crotalus adamanteus) *is unique to the Southeast. It is the largest of the rattlers and the most dangerous because of the noxious strength of its venom.*

In the style of Charles Bird King, 1826.

SEMINOLE

♦ Their name is perhaps the translation of the Creek term "fugitive." It is probably a corruption of the Spanish *cimarron*, "wild." They called themselves *ikaniuksalgi*, "people of the peninsula."

♦ Language: Muskogean.

♦ They settled in Florida.

♦ They were farmers who raised corn, squash, tobacco, sweet potatoes, and melons, and hunters, fishermen, and fruit gatherers. They also raised cattle abandoned by the Spanish.

♦ An ethnically-mixed people, as a result of successive influxes of tribes (Yamassee, Apalachee, Creek, and Red Stick), the Seminole fled from the invasions of Whites and Black slaves. The Seminole were forced to leave Florida from 1817 to 1858 after three wars against the Americans. Except for 300 Seminole who refused to leave the Everglades, the others went into exile.

♦ In 1970, there were about 4,000 Seminole in Oklahoma and 2,000 in Florida.

Seminole shelter.

The raccoon (procyon lotor) *is an indigenous American animal. Omnivorous, living in wooded areas, along rivers and lakes, the raccoon lives a sedentary life around its den, usually a hollow tree trunk. It interrupts its habits only during mating, when the male leaves to find a companion with whom he shares a few days before leaving in search of new adventures.*

From a photo in *Harper's Weekly*, 1858.

THE GREAT FOREST

The French and the English set foot in this region during the sixteenth century. They discovered a vast land covered with thick forests, diffused with a dense network of rivers and lakes. The village settlements were usually located near water and some cleared areas for growing corn or tobacco. There was an abundance of fish and a wide variety of game proliferated from the undergrowth to the treetops. Each spring, the people gathered maple sap. The liquid was stored in bark buckets often made of birch. Burning stones were dropped into the buckets to bring the syrup to a boil. The syrup was a common staple of the Northeast diet.

Fishermen, hunters, and also farmers, the Native people found all the necessary material in the immense forest to make weapons and utensils for building houses and palisades to protect the villages. To facilitate felling the trees, some were burned. Then the men cut, hollowed, and sanded the wood with the aid of tools made of stone, bone, or shell. They stripped bark from trees, flattened and cut the bark into sheets, and used them to cover the walls and roofs of community houses and to make canoes. The longest and most supple wood fibers were used to make bindings and nets. Like their brothers on the continent, the tribes from the forest areas knew how to make the best use of their natural environment.

These are the men the French, followed by the English some years later, first encountered. Some Northeastern people wore headdresses made of feathers, their faces and bodies painted in brilliant colors. Reports from outsiders expressed astonishment: "Nose painted in blue...eyebrows and cheeks in black...red, blue, black stripes from the mouth to the ears...the face entirely black except the forehead, the perimeter of the ears and the chin...a black or red band from one ear to the other...face half-green, half-red...." The paintings, combined with tattoos, were sometimes applied to boys and girls at puberty. The tattoos were usually an invocation of protective powers—animals or natural forces—revealed by visions or in dreams. In certain tribes, like the Neutral of Lake Erie, tattoos covered the whole body in a sort of decorative frenzy.

In this vast region (1,800 miles [3,000 km] from east to west and 1,200 miles [2,000 km] from north to south), the majority of tribes spoke Algonquian languages. The exceptions were the Winnebago, who spoke a Siouan language and lived on the banks of Lake Michigan, and the Nations of the Iroquois tribes, who settled to the east and south of Lake Ontario. Another people who spoke the Iroquoian language were the Tuscarora, who lived on the Atlantic coast of what is today North Carolina. ▲

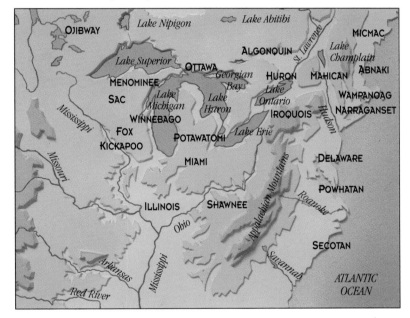

Plentiful throughout North America, beavers lived in swamps and near lakes and small rivers. Willows, birch, aspens, and maples provided them with food and construction material. The beaver's fur was the most important trade item with Europeans at the beginning of the seventeenth century and for centuries beyond.

IN THE NAME OF THE "VIRGIN QUEEN"

In the style of John White, 1590.

SECOTAN

♦ Their name means, "there where it is burned," perhaps a reference to this farming people's technique of clearing by fire.

♦ Language: Algonquian.

♦ They inhabited the coast of North Carolina between the Albermarle and Pamlico Bays.

♦ Farmers of primarily corn, beans, and squash, they were also hunters and fishermen. Their villages near the sea were surrounded by palisades and contained ten to thirty large houses.

♦ Their life was described by John White, who accompanied Sir Walter Raleigh. Like their neighbors the Powhatan, they were overwhelmed by the European colonists in the seventeenth century. The Machapunga, Pamlico, and Hattera, who lived in the region afterward, appear to have been descendants of the Secotan.

In the style of John White, 1590.

Secotan house.

From the North to the South, from the Tuscarora territories to the banks of present-day New Hampshire, the Algonquian tribes (Secotan, Powhatan, Nanticoke, Delaware, Mohegan, Narragansett, Wampanoag, Massachusett, Abenaki, and many, many others), who shared the coastal areas, existed upon resources from the forest, fertile coastal plain, and the ocean with its inexhaustible resources of fish and shellfish.

The Northeast Coast was "conquered" first by the English. Sir Walter Raleigh arrived in 1584 and sent Arthur Barlow to explore the back country. They took possession of the region and called it Virginia in honor of their sovereign, Elizabeth I, the "Virgin Queen." Barlow encountered Indian people on his journey and wrote: "They are very friendly people, hospitable, without ruse or deception. They seem to live in a golden age of their history." In spite of these good omens, two attempts at colonization ended in failure. John White, commissioned by Raleigh to locate his former companions in the territory of neighboring tribes, realized they had vanished. Raleigh had left behind a new colony of 122 men at Roanoke.

When Raleigh and John White returned in 1590, the colony had mysteriously disappeared, and no one knew what had happened to the men. John White never saw his companions again, but he left a series of drawings, documenting the life of the Secotan and the organization of their villages.

In 1607, a new colony of 144 English settled on the Powhatan territory. They were ordered "to not disturb the natives," but their religious fanaticism, their greed, and the brutality of the settlers quickly aroused the hostility of the Indians. In spite of John Smith's marriage to Pocahontas, chief Powhatan's daughter, the years that followed witnessed a succession of blood and treacherous episodes. The expansion of the colony was made at the price of the destruction of the confederation and led to the disappearance of the tribes that were a part of it. ▲

Based on a watercolor by John White, this sixteenth-century illustration portrays an Algonquian village on the coast of Virginia.

A. *Proximity to water.*
B. *Cornfield with lookout in the shelter.*
C. *Communal habitation with mat coverings.*
D. *Vegetable gardens.*
E. *Villagers eating a meal.*
F. *Fire near a place of worship.*
G. *Ritual dance around masks of effigy figures.*

In the style of Wencelaus Hollar, 1645.

POWHATAN

♦ The Powhatan were a confederation of tribes under the authority of Wahunsonacock, chief of the Potomac (Pamukey, Rappahannock, Nansemond, Mattapony, and many other tribes). Europeans used the name Powhatan, which was accepted by Native people to designate the groups of this confederation.

♦ Language: Algonquian.

♦ They inhabited the coast of Virginia and Maryland.

♦ They were farmers and hunters.

♦ Between 1607, when Jamestown was founded, and 1675, there were a succession of uninterrupted truces and massacres between Europeans and the Powhatan. Within sixty years, the Powhatan confederacy was reduced to a few small groups.

♦ Some descendants live in Virginia today.

MIDCOASTAL TRIBES

In the style of Peter Martensen Lindstrom, 1653

A typical example of an Algonquian community, the Delaware were the largest tribe in their immediate area; they were located in parts of present-day Pennsylvania, New Jersey, and New York. Their communities were not monolithic, but rather groups of related tribes, each led by a *sachem* whose political powers were limited but who had great wisdom. A council of elders that included the sachem often made group decisions. At his death, the sachem was often replaced by his nearest relation on the female side (his sister's son, for example). The Delaware system of government and political power were passed on through the female line. However, men usually assumed economic, religious, or political responsibilities for the communities and their families.

Often located along or near riverbeds, Delaware villages were composed of buildings of various sizes, from the round single-family bark-covered home to the much larger communal house referred to as a longhouse. The Delaware honored many different spiritual forces that related to nature and communicated with men through natural phenomena. The spiritual forces were everywhere, influencing each being and every thing.

DELAWARE

♦ Named after Lord de La Warr, first European governor of Virginia. The Delaware called themselves *lenni* or *lenapes*, the "ordinary, real person."

♦ Language: Algonquian.

♦ They lived in the states of Delaware, New Jersey, New York, and eastern Pennsylvania during early historic times.

♦ They were hunters, fishermen, and farmers. Respected by other Algonquian Nations because of their confederacy, the group was really a council of about 200 elders (called "the Old and Wise Men of the Nation"). By 1750, the Delaware emerged with three large family units, *tukwsi-t* (the wolf), *pele'* (the turkey), and *pukuwanku* (the turtle).

♦ After a rough start with the Dutch, the Delaware chief Tammady signed a treaty with William Penn in 1683 that introduced an era of peace lasting over 50 years. But the Delaware lost their most fruitful lands in the "Walking Purchase" (1737) and left for the Susquehanna (PA) and Ohio River Valleys.

♦ As the Delaware were pushed west by European expansionism, some groups participated in the last revolts in the East under Little Turtle in 1790 and Tecumseh in 1812. In the Civil War, the Delaware fought with the Union.

♦ Today, two areas in Oklahoma contain small Delaware communities (Bartlesville/Copan and Anadarko) and there is one community in upstate New York, near the Six Nations reservations.

Water game was plentiful in the Northeastern states, a region rich in lakes and rivers, situated on the axis of migration between northern Canada and the Gulf of Mexico. Among others, three birds were favorite targets of hunters.

A. The Canadian goose (branta canadensis).

B. The mallard (anas platyrhynchos).

C. The wood duck (aix sponsa).

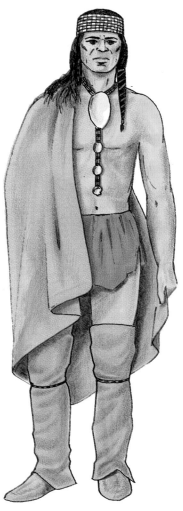

Based on a portrait by John Winthrop, 1637.

NARRAGANSETT

♦ Called the "people of the little island."

♦ Language: Algonquian.

♦ They lived in Rhode Island and Connecticut.

♦ They were farmers.

♦ They helped defeat their enemies, the Pequots, and were the most powerful tribe in northeastern New England in 1637. The Narragansett were defeated in King Philips' war (1675). Survivors joined the Niantic or fled New England.

♦ Twenty-five Narragansett were counted in 1900. Descendants live in Rhode Island on an 1,800-acre, federally recognized reservation.

WAMPANOAG

♦ The derivation unknown but in the Delaware language it may mean "people to the east."

♦ Language: Algonquian.

♦ They lived in present-day Massachusetts and Rhode Island.

♦ They were farmers and fishermen.

♦ Massasoit, their chief, helped the Mayflower Pilgrims in 1621. The settlement of the colonists was at the expense of other tribes.

♦ Massasoit died in 1662. His eldest son whom the Whites called King Philip, succeeded him. In 1675 and 1676, he led a bloody war against the colonists and their allies, the Mohegan. Killed in 1676, his Nation was then divided. Some of the survivors were sold as slaves.

In the style of Cyrus Dallin.

These Algonquian people frequently visited neighbors to barter goods. Their transactions took place in a friendly atmosphere where they often showed their mutual trust by smoking tobacco together for awhile.

Conflicts did occur among these tribes, sometimes reflecting their concern for preserving their identity and freedom more than to dominate and conquer. ▲

Maple syrup was an important food supplement for Native Americans, and its harvest, in the spring, was a significant event marked during the year. A hole bored into a maple tree's trunk allowed the sap to flow and run into bark buckets, often made of birch, the sap was then boiled in large cauldrons until it was very thick.

BETWEEN THE HUDSON AND ST. LAWRENCE

Further north, the Micmac, Malecite, Abenaki, Pennacook, and others lived in present-day Maine, a mountainous region exposed to the cold winds from Labrador and not adapted to agriculture. Often moving from one season to the next, the Native people of this region built temporary housing from tree bark. Usually, these were single-family dwellings made from several young trees stacked and covered with bark, often from the birch trees. Despite the colder climate, the people moved to an environment with more abundant natural resources when they needed food—utilizing lake and river fish and a multitude of geese, ducks, and beavers.

The moose was a favorite hunting game and provided an important supply of meat and hides. Hunting techniques often varied according to the season. Game was generally either trapped with a net or shot with an arrow. In the fall, moose were either drawn into the arrow's shooting range by the use of a decoy or a mating call. The elk hunters of the Great Forest and the subarctic region also used this method. In winter, the moose, like buffalo, had trouble moving around in the deep snow. Wearing snowshoes, hunters were able to approach animals at close range. ▲

Hunting moose in winter.

MICMAC

♦ The tribal name, *mi-kemaw*, may mean "allies," or it may have a geographical significance. People called themselves *elnu*, "Indian."

♦ Language: Algonquian.

♦ In the 16th century, they occupied the area south and west of the Gulf of St. Lawrence.

♦ They were hunters, allied with the Abenaki.

♦ They were probably seen by John Cabot along the coast in 1497. Jacques Cartier encountered the Micmac in the St. Lawrence Gulf in 1534. They approached him with furs as welcoming gifts, but he chased them with canon fire.

♦ Allied with the French, they delayed the settlement of the English in Nova Scotia and New Brunswick, after helping eliminate the Beothuk Indians from Newfoundland in 1706.

♦ The Micmac people live in Canada and Maine with a population today of over 12,000.

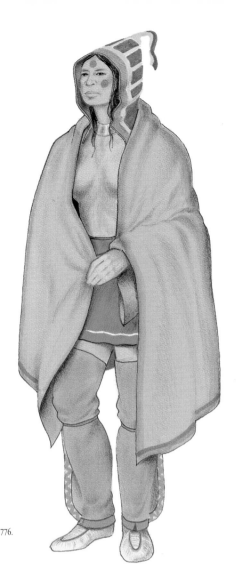

Based on a watercolor, 1776.

ABENAKI

♦ From the Abenaki word, *wapanahki*, "Dawn Land People."

♦ Language: Algonquian.

♦ They inhabited present-day southern Maine, most of New Hampshire, and Vermont.

♦ Brave warriors, the Abenaki formed a confederation of tribes (Penobscot, Pennacook, and others) to oppose the French presence in 1755. Many Abenaki were converted to Christianity by the Jesuits during the 17th century.

♦ Allied with the French, they waged an intense war against the English, who took revenge by massacring a community founded by Father Sebastien Rale in Norridgewock in 1724.

♦ Weakened by war and smallpox, the Abenaki surrendered their weapons in 1754. Seven hundred of them, however, fought with the Americans in the Revolutionary War.

♦ Their descendants, around 1,800 people, live in Quebec and Maine.

From the description by a Dutch colonist in the beginning of the eighteenth century.

MAHICAN

♦ According to oral traditions, the name is from "Muhheakunnuk," the name of a local area, referring to the tidewater of the Hudson River near Albany, New York. Other Native people of the region interpreted the name *Mahican* as an Algonquian word meaning "wolves."

♦ Language: Algonquian.

♦ They lived along the banks of the Hudson River, through northern New York state.

♦ Farmers, hunters, and fishermen, their way of life was like that of the Delaware and Mohegan.

♦ They fought the Mohawks for control of the Hudson fur trade. At the beginning of the 18th century, the English colonists drove them from their land. Like the majority of Algonquian, they sided with the French. Some fought under General Lafayette in the American Revolution.

♦ Today there is a reservation in Wisconsin.

The moose is the largest animal of the deer family. It can reach the height of a horse, and its antlers may span more than four feet (1.5 m) in width. Living in the woods, it is particularly fond of marshes and groves. In the summer, moose often search alone for food, eating mostly willow leaves and aquatic plants. In the winter, they travel in small herds, eating twigs and birch bark.

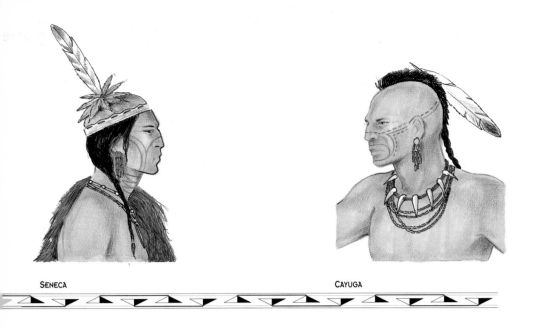

SENECA

CAYUGA

ONONDAGA

THE LEAGUE OF
FIVE NATIONS

In the style of Benjamin West, 1759.

The territories of the five original Nations of the League of the Iroquois are fanned out to the south of Lake Ontario and located in what is now upstate New York. From west to east, these Nations are the Seneca, Cayuga, Onondaga, Oneida, and Mohawk. This is an area where the Finger Lakes region are set in the wooded and fertile hills, close to the vestiges of the last glaciation or ice age. Were the Iroquois the first inhabitants of this region or did they arrive as intruders and settle in a world already inhabited by Algonquian-speaking Native people? If the first hypothesis seems the most plausible for archaeologists, the second appeals to certain linguists who suggest a possible relationship between the Iroquoian and Caddoan dialect from the Western Plains.

The Five Nations joined together to form the most powerful tribal government in North America. It is unknown precisely when or where the Iroquois Nations formed their union, but according to tradition, the formation occurred during the fifteenth century. Traditional history states that a wise man, Deganawidah, had the dream of ending the wars that had caused the death of so many Indian men. Another Iroquoian, Hiawatha, convinced the Nations to unite their forces instead of fighting. The resulting confederation gave strength to Iroquoian warriors who affirmed their supremacy over their neighbors, especially those who spoke languages relating to their own, including the Erie, the Neutral, and the Tabac. Even the powerful Huron yielded to confederacy raids. The dominant power in a strategic region, the Iroquois, from the seventeenth century on, attempted and succeeded in controlling the fur trade. They played a key role in the war between the French and the English.

The Iroquois lived in large bark-covered houses, called "longhouses," which were shared by several related family groups. The large homes were grouped into villages, usually protected by palisades, and often situated on hills near water sources. Surrounding areas were cleared and cultivated. Every fifteen or twenty years, a village was moved as local natural resources diminished.

Women played an important role in the community; for example, they owned most of the property, including the homes. They were responsible for agricultural tasks, including the harvesting of corn, squash, or beans, and for stocking reserves in silos that were dug into the ground and lined with grass and bark. Women raised the children and took care of the elderly. Female lineage was also the basis for social and political organization.

ONEIDA

MOHAWK

TUSCARORA

IROQUOIS

♦ Their name comes from an Algonquian term, *irocois*, first recorded in use by Algonquian-speaking people around the St. Lawrence River. The Iroquois call themselves *ho-de-no-sau-nee*, "people of the longhouse."

♦ The League of Five Nations combined groups from west to east:
Seneca—*onotowa-ka*, "people of the big hill."
Cayuga—*kayohkho-nq*, "people of the place where the boats were taken out," the boats referring to a town named Oioguen.
Onondaga—*onota-ke-ka*, "people from the hill."
Oneida—*oneyote-a-ka*, "people of the erected stone."
Mohawk—From *Mohowawogs*, a Narragansett or Massachusett word meaning "eaters of men." The Mohawk call themselves kanye-keha-ka, "people of the gun flint."

♦ The Iroquois Confederacy increased from five to six Nations with the arrival of the Tuscarora (*skaro-re*, "those of the Indian hemp") from the South about 1722.

♦ Language: Iroquoian.

♦ They settled along the southern banks of Lake Ontario.

♦ They were farmers, hunters, and exceptional warriors and businessmen in the fur trade. The Six Nations worship a complex group of spirits reflecting animals, plants, and natural forces.

♦ The Grand Council unites 50 *sachems*, or chiefs: 8 Seneca, 10 Cayuga, 14 Onondaga, 9 Oneida, and 9 Mohawk. In reality, only 8 Mohawk took their council seats, no one replacing Hiawatha, the founder of the League.

♦ Until the end of the eighteenth century, the Iroquois took part in nearly all the European wars. Allied with the English against the French, their participation was crucial. Under the leadership of Mohawk Joseph Brant, they remained faithful to their allies against the insurgent Americans during the Revolutionary War; only the Oneida chose neutrality. When they were defeated, many of their villages were destroyed in 1779.

♦ Reservations in New York state were set aside for the Six Nations, also in Wisconsin (Oneida), Oklahoma (Seneca), and Canada (Mohawk).

Iroquois club.

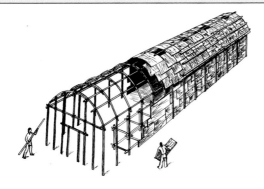

Building of an Iroquois house.

Women appointed the chiefs representing the Nations at the Grand Council, the highest authority of the League. Some leaders were chosen from among the male descendants of the mothers of the first chiefs Hiawatha had selected.

The annual round of ceremonies, which marked communal life, was tied to the rhythms of the seasons and to the crops (apple, corn, or strawberry festivals that are expressions of gratitude to the nourishing earth), or to celebrations by religious societies, whose goal was to heal (False Face societies) and predict the future. ▲

In the style of Langdon Kihn, end of the eighteenth century.

ON THE SHORES OF THE NORTHERN GREAT LAKES

Based on an etching, 1847.

HURON

♦ They called themselves *ouendat* or *wendat*, "people of the peninsula." There are close variations in the *Guyandot* or *Wyandot* language. French explorer Samuel Champlain and his companions called these people the Huron because of their boar's headdress.

♦ Language: Iroquoian.

♦ They settled between Lake Huron and Lake Ontario.

♦ They farmed corn, wheat, beans, sunflower; fished; and hunted.

♦ They lived in villages built by a lake or river, in longhouses made of elm bark.

♦ Their eight social clans (Turtle, Wolf, Bear, Beaver, Deer, Hawk, Porcupine, and Snake), were organized into four political units as a confederation. With conversion to Christianity through missionaries, the Huron allied with France. The Iroquois, used this as a pretext to destroy them in 1648.

♦ Some descendants live today on the Wyandot reservation in Oklahoma. Another community is located in Lorette, Quebec.

In the style of Samuel Champlain, 1615.

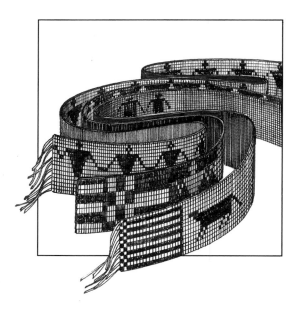

One way of celebrating an event or recording it was to weave a special item called a wampum *(an abbreviation of the Algonquian* wampumpeag) *belt, made of fragments of cylindrical seashell beads woven together in the form of a long, rectangular, "belt-like" item or an individual string of beads. These had considerable value and were also used to mark mourning and condolences at the time of a death. The beads also served as a type of currency for the European colonists during the fur trade when they ran out of metal coins.*

The region encompassed by Lakes Ontario, Erie, Huron, and Simcoe, was a fertile enclave with open hills irrigated by a number of ponds and rivers. This vast territory belonged to other tribes, the Huron being the most prominent, who spoke an Iroquoian language. They had many things in common with the Six Nations, such as similar habitat, crops, and tribal organization.

When Samuel Champlain encountered them in 1609, the Huron saw an alliance with the French as a way to balance the threat the Iroquois Confederacy posed as middlemen in the European fur trade. Their loyalty to this alliance was a significant factor in their ultimate decline.

Champlain, who stayed several months among the Huron, made many sketches and observations of them. He noticed that the people practiced a form of hunting that reminded him of the "beautiful country of France." Hunters tramped noisily in the woods, driving the game toward an enclosure where the animals were trapped and then caught.

Champlain was also impressed by the Huron rituals, especially the great Feast of the Dead, which was held every ten to twelve years. When a person died, rituals accompanied the dead, but every decade or so, the bodies were unearthed by family members for a special ceremony lasting several days. The ceremony symbolized a tribal union between political factions. The flesh of all but the most recently buried was removed from the bodies. Grave effects were elaborate and many were saved to be given to the people in attendance. Bodies were brought to one location from the many villages for the ceremonies. A large pit was carved and lined with beaver furs. Upon a signal, families threw and/or dropped the bones of their relatives plus decorations from the grave into the pit. The grave was covered with mats, bark, and a layer of sand. Feasting and celebrating followed.

The Huron believed this was the way the souls of the departed traveled toward the spiritual world of the dead, a place where men and women could resume their traditional activities of hunting, fishing, and farming.

In the style of Sir Joshua Jebb, 1815.

OTTAWA

♦ Their name for themselves is *ota-wa*.

♦ Language: Algonquian.

♦ They lived on the banks of the Georgian Bay and on Manitoulin Island, north of Lake Huron.

♦ They took part in the traditional activities of the Great Lakes Algonquians. The Ottawa served as middlemen from East to West.

♦ Driven by Iroquoian groups to northern Lake Michigan, they were loyal allies of the French. After the Treaty of Paris (1763), their chief, Pontiac, refused to accept English rule and continued the struggle.

♦ The Ottawa were part of the Federation of United Indian Nations under Mohawk Joseph Brant, who was hostile to American expansion. But the Ottawa ceded their land to the federal government by way of treaties in 1785, 1789, 1795, and 1836.

♦ Some of the tribe lives today on a reservation in Oklahoma and many others settled in Michigan and Ontario. The recent total population figure for these three areas is 8,000.

Other Nations living in the area were neighbors of the Huron and allied against the Iroquois, the common enemy. To the north were the Algonquins (who gave their name to the linguistic family, Algonquian), and to the south, the Ottawa, who lived on the banks of Georgia. The two tribes shared the same way of life through farming, fishing, and hunting. Tribes from throughout the area moved several times annually. They traveled in a perimeter of thirty to seventy-five miles (100 km) around a main village to hunt game. They lived in the main village during the summer, women working the fields while men hunted small game in the nearby forest. Fish was an important part of their diet. Birch bark canoes were essential to explore the lakes and the streams. ▲

ALGONQUIN

♦ The name is a derivative of the Malecite dialect, *elakomkwik*, "they are our relatives or allies." Another interpretation finds the origin of the name in the Micmac language, *algoomeaking*, "they harpoon fish." Champlain called them *Algoumequin*, and the Iroquois *Adirondack*, "eaters of trees."

♦ Their language is Algonquian, from which their name is derived. Note the different spelling for the tribal name, well accepted by current-day scholars.

♦ They occupied the northern part of the St. Lawrence River and Lake Huron to the east of Montreal and both banks of the Ottawa River.

♦ They lived in bands of several hundred people, divided into hunting groups. They were also fishermen and farmers and lived in large wood houses made of birch bark.

♦ They became faithful allies of the French soon after they encountered Champlain in 1603. They waged consistent war with the Iroquois.

♦ Four to five thousand Algonquin live in eastern Toronto and western Quebec.

Based on an anonymous sketch, 1774.

On the Shores of the Western Great Lakes

The Ojibwa occupied the north bank of Lake Superior and profited from the riches of the forest and the waters. Near Green Bay, northeast of Lake Michigan, the Menominee were an exception. More sedentary than their neighbors, their lives largely focused upon sturgeon fishing and wild rice harvesting. The rice was harvested from a kind of grass that grows abundantly in the muddy waters of rivers and lakes. The harvest was made in canoes at the end of summer. A man steered the boat into the tall grass and two women, grabbing an armful of grass in passing, hit the tops of the plants, making the grain fall to the bottom of the canoe.

The Menominee harvested more rice than they could eat. It served as trading currency with the Winnebago, their nearest neighbors, with whom, in spite of the difference in language, they had cordial relations. In exchange for the Menominee's rice, the Winnebago, who were skillful farmers, offered them their harvest surplus of corn and tobacco. They would also offer to exchange buffalo hides. Winnebago people traveled onto the plains to hunt buffalo. The alliance between the Menominee and the Winnebago was also a means of controlling the Sac and Fox in the Southeast. ▲

OJIBWA

♦ Also called Chippewa in areas of the United States, they called themselves anissina-pe, meaning "Indian" or "human being." For the Cree, they were the "men who spoke the same language." For the Huron, "the men of the falls." For the French, the "Saulteaux" (allusion to the Sault Sainte Marie Falls).

♦ Language: Algonquian.

♦ Like the Cree, the Ojibwa were divided into plains and forest tribes; the latter occupied the north bank of Lake Superior.

♦ They were mobile hunters, notable as fishermen and canoe builders. Their birch bark dwellings were built by both men and women.

♦ They were active participants in the fur trade. They were allied with the Ottawa and Potawatomi, especially against the Fox. They fought on the side of the English against the insurgent Americans and participated in revolts led by Little Turtle in 1790 and Tecumseh in 1812.

♦ Estimated at 30,000 in 1905, the Ojibwa population lives today around the American-Canadian border with about half on reservations.

One of the largest tribes in North America, there are estimated to be more than 75,000 Ojibwa/Chippewa today.

In the style of Peter Rindisbacher, 1821.

Ojibwa tepee.

Wild rice harvest.

This aquatic plant is the zizania aquatica. *It grows in stagnant waters bordering Lakes Superior and Michigan. For the people of the region, the plant constituted an essential part of their food supply. The harvest was made in canoes at the end of summer. During the operation, a large number of grain fell into the water, thus assuring future germination. The harvest was dried in the sun, and the wind took care of the winnowing. Wild rice was boiled and eaten, often with maple syrup.*

WINNEBAGO

♦ From an Algonquian language, possibly Potawatomi, the name is from *winpyeko*, "people of the dirty water," a reference to the muddy water of the Fox River and Lake Winnebago. They called themselves *hochangara*, "people of the true word," from the belief that they were one of the founding tribes of the Sioux.

♦ Language: Siouan.

♦ They lived north of the west bank of Lake Michigan (Door Peninsula and Green Bay).

♦ They were buffalo hunters and also cultivated and farmed corn, tobacco, beans, and squash. Their customs and beliefs were similar to those of the Sioux in the Dakotas.

♦ Allied with the French, then with the English, the Winnebago opposed the Americans until the end of the Black Hawk Revolt in 1832. Many were decimated by illness and epidemics.

♦ The Winnebago reservation in Nebraska is also shared with the Omaha.

In the style of George Catlin, 1835.

In the style of George Catlin, 1831.

MENOMINEE

♦ Their full name, *me'nome'ne*, is derived from the Ojibwa, meaning "wild rice people."

♦ Language: Algonquian.

♦ They inhabited a territory located between Lake Michigan and Lake Superior.

♦ Mainly sedentary, they were, despite language differences, allied with the Winnebago in order to contain their enemies, the Sac and Fox.

♦ Fishing in the waters of the Great Lakes, they gathered wild rice and harvested maple syrup. The women were noted for their skillful weaving. Using vegetable fibers and buffalo skins, they made bags and ribbons.

♦ French explorer Jean Nicollet encountered them in 1634. The Menominee participated in the Pontiac Revolt in 1763, afterward becoming neutral.

♦ Today, about 6,400 Menominee live in Wisconsin on tribal lands.

On the Shores of Lake Michigan

Fox

♦ A name given by Whites in reference to Red Fox, one of their family clans. They call themselves *meskwahki-haki*, meaning "Red Earths."

♦ Language: Algonquian.

♦ They settled east of Lake Michigan, south of the Sac territory. They were farmers and buffalo hunters who moved seasonally. They were in a constant state of warfare with the Ojibwa and others in the region.

♦ In contact with Europeans since 1660, they favored the English against the French, who wanted to trade with their Sioux enemies. With their population dwindling, they merged with their Sac neighbors, with whom they had many things in common.

♦ Today, they live on Oklahoma reservations, with the Sac, and in Iowa. In 1955, their population was estimated at about 650.

In the style of Charles Bird King, 1837.

Sac

♦ They call themselves *asa-ki-waki*, "Yellow Earths." They were mentioned in 1640 by the Jesuits under the Huron name *Hvattoghronon*, meaning "people of the setting sun." They had been known as *Sauk* but prefer *Sac*.

♦ Language: Algonquian.

♦ They lived on western Lake Michigan, the eastern part of what is now the state of Wisconsin.

♦ They were farmers and buffalo hunters like their allies, the Fox. They were considered among the most aggressive people of the Great Lakes region.

♦ They sided with no European powers but took part in revolts by Pontiac in 1763 and by Tecumseh, between 1801 and 1814. The Sac signed a treaty in 1815 that confirmed the loss of their territory. The final revolt in 1842 failed under the leadership of their chief, Black Hawk.

♦ Their descendants live on reservations in Oklahoma, Kansas, and Iowa with the Fox. The 1950 population figure for the Oklahoma Sac was 996. Recent figures for the Kansas Sac and Fox are 300.

Sac winter shelter.

In the style of George Catlin, 1835.

The Sac, Fox, and Kickapoo, who live in present-day Wisconsin, like their neighbors traveled seasonally, combining farming and buffalo hunting. All were formidable warriors, but the Sac and Fox were constantly at war with the Ojibwa/Chippewa. Battles were not fought between armies European-style; their wars were encounters between small groups of warriors eager to settle an offense or to prove their courage. The return of a victorious warrior was celebrated with ritual ceremonies such as the *Misekwe*, the Scalp Dance. Occasionally, scalps were taken and brought back to the chief of the village. Once trophies were collected, the dance began and each warrior told the story of his battle. Exaggeration was received with contempt by the other warriors. An extraordinary exploit, such as an encounter with a group of enemies and contact with a chief on the arm or hand might lead to the warrior's receiving a new name that expressed his bravery.

Other ceremonies marked the life of many of the Great Lakes tribes. In the seventeenth century, the *Midewiwin*, or Medicine Dance, was recorded and known to be practiced by tribes throughout the region. These rites invoked forces capable of conquering illness and of assuring a peaceful journey to the world beyond for all those who belonged to the society. During the initiation rite, a candidate received cowrie shells on a piece of leather to wear at all times. The shells were contained in a medicine bag made of otter skin and they were thrown into the initiate's lap. Those who were struck believed that the shell entered their bodies and cured them of illness. They fell to the ground as if dead and then rose to the dawn of a new life. ▲

POTAWATOMI

♦ Their name is from the Ojibwa *po-te-wa-tami*. It has no known meaning. The common translation of "men of the place of the fire" is a misnomer.

♦ Language: Algonquian

♦ They occupied the east bank of Lake Michigan.

♦ Moving seasonally, they were hunters and fishermen. They practiced night fishing by placing fires at the bow of their boats.

♦ Allied with the French against the English, they participated in the Pontiac Revolt in 1763. They settled in Indiana and opposed American colonization. Expelled in 1846, they settled in Kansas, where they clashed with the Pawnee.

♦ Their descendants live on reservations in OK (4,000) and KS (14,000+). Some have returned to the southern Great Lakes.

In the style of Paul Kane, 1845.

KICKAPOO

♦ Their name comes from *kiikaapoa*, meaning unknown. The commonly mistaken interpretation of another spelling, *ki-wika-pa-wa*, as "he is around here," is not accurate. The Tonkawa people called them "deer eaters," and the Huron, *ontarahronon*, "lake people."

♦ Language: Algonquian.

♦ They settled in the southern part of Lake Michigan's west bank.

♦ Formidable warriors, they were called "handsome, proud, and very independent."

♦ Marquette and Joliet encountered them in 1672. The Kickapoo participated in the Pontiac Revolt (1763) and the victory of the Maumee over the Americans (1790), followed by Tecumseh's revolt. They played an important part in the Black Hawk Revolt in 1832. Exiled to the South, they settled in Texas with the Delaware and Cherokee. They were allies of the Mexicans in their attempt to reconquer Texas in 1839. Part of the Kickapoo tribe went into exile in Mexico in order to protect the border from Apache and Comanche raids.

♦ There are Kickapoo lands in Oklahoma, Kansas, Texas, and Mexico. There are 1,500 Kickapoo in Kansas. The Texas tribe has just gained federal recognition; no figures are available.

In the style of August Schoeft, 1865.

OHIO VALLEY ALGONQUIAN

MIAMI

♦ Their name is from the Algonquian Ojibwa name, *oma-mi*, with no known translation. Miami tradition refers to their name as "twaatwaa," an imitation of a call of the cranes.

♦ Language: Algonquian.

♦ They were mobile farmers and buffalo hunters. Originally from Wisconsin, they occupied present-day northern Indiana and Illinois and were comprised of more or less independent tribes (Wea, Piankashaw, etc.).

♦ After the departure of their French allies, they survived attacks by Joseph Brant, Tecumseh, and Little Turtle (the latter himself of the Miami tribe), struggling against the conquest of their land.

♦ About 350 descendants live on an Oklahoma reservation, with 700 counted in Indiana in 1950.

In the style of George Catlin, 1830.

In the style of Gwillim Simloe, 1790.

Buffalo hunt.

To the south of Lake Michigan, in present-day Indiana and Illinois, there were other tribes who spoke the Algonquian language—the Miami and Illinois people, practicing agriculture and hunting buffalo like their neighbors in the North.

In the southern region of the Great Forest, occupying the rich Ohio Valley, the Shawnee were mainly farmers. They had good relations with the Delaware in the East and with the Creek to the South.

After choosing to ally themselves with the French, like other Algonquian tribes, the Shawnee were caught in a tide of unending wars that bloodied the eastern part of the country. The English colonists pushed the Native Americans of the North Atlantic coast to the Ohio Valley. Then, from the beginning of the nineteenth century, through the same valley, Americans began to settle lands toward the Mississippi. This second wave forced the Shawnee to abandon their land, and like their Native American brothers, to flee westward, toward exile and decline. ▲

ILLINOIS

♦ Their name is of uncertain origin. The term *iliniwek* has been widely used in early literature but its translation is also unknown.

♦ Language: Algonquian.

♦ They lived along the western border of what is the present state of Illinois. Most tribal settlements were scattered along the Illinois River.

♦ Farmers, hunters, gatherers, they formed a group of language-related tribes with the Peoria, Kaskaskia, Tamaroa, Cahokia, Michigamea, Moingwena, etc. There is no evidence of a political organization, such as a confederacy.

♦ Allied with the French, they were crushed by the Five Nations Iroquois in 1684. When the great Ottawa chief, Pontiac, was killed by an Illinois in 1769, the Kickapoo declared war. Only a few hundred Illinois survived.

♦ After selling their land, they went into exile in Kansas. In 1854, a treaty grouped the Peoria, Kaskaskia, Miami, Wea, and Piankashaw tribes on an Oklahoma reservation. Population figures were estimated at about 200.

In the style of George Catlin, 1830.

In the style of Joseph Wabin, 1796.

SHAWNEE

♦ Their name is probably borrowed by the French from the Ottawa. The earliest reference seems to be *sa-wanwa*, "person of the south."

♦ Language: Algonquian.

♦ By the end of the 18th century, their encampments were mainly in the Ohio River Valley, which was probably their pre-European contact home. At the end of the 17th century, they were scattered in Illinois, Ohio, and Maryland.

♦ Hunters, farmers, and food gatherers, their villages were well organized and contained a central council house.

♦ They steadfastly defended their territory, first against the English, then later against the Americans. Chief Tecumseh defeated the Americans at the battle of the Wabash on November 4, 1791. Under the leadership of General Anthony Wayne, the Americans won revenge at the battle of Fallen Timbers. In spite of the prophecies of Tenskwatawa, Tecumseh's brother, also called the Shawnee Prophet, the Shawnee were dispersed in the early part of the nineteenth century and were scattered throughout the region in Kansas, Missouri, Texas, and Oklahoma.

♦ Descendants live on a reservation in Oklahoma (pop. 2,600).

THE GREAT PLAINS

The Great Plains is a vast area in the center of North America that stretches from the southern part of present-day Canadian Alberta, Saskatchewan, and Manitoba to the Gulf of Mexico. It is bound on the east by the Mississippi River Valley and on the west by the Rocky Mountains, an area almost five times as large as the state of Texas. In this immense region, there are two main geographic environments—the more fertile tall grass areas of Missouri, Iowa, and Arkansas, and the arid short grassland regions of Texas, Kansas, and Colorado.

Before Europeans arrived in the area, Native people were primarily agricultural and the region was probably sparsely populated. The buffalo was not the mainstay of life. After the introduction of horses and guns, the buffalo became the dominant means of subsistence and populations living on or near the Plains borders moved out onto the Plains to hunt. Buffalo numbered more than 25 million during much of the nineteenth century and they migrated annually to the West and North in the spring, and to the East and South in the fall. Many Native people followed the herds.

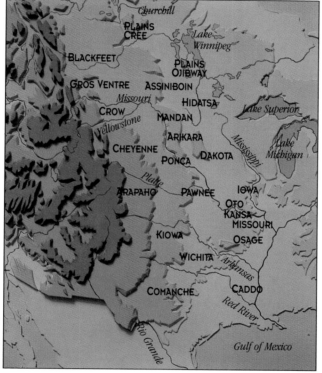

bones for tools, tendons and fat for food and all manner of community survival. Buffalo hunting afforded young warriors the opportunity to perfect the making and handling of weapons, to develop their warrior skills, and to test their courage—hunting was an occasion that helped transform a hunter into a warrior. ▲

Buffalo were trapped in a simple and effective manner prior to the introduction of horses. Hunters frightened herds toward an incline or to the edge of a cliff. The animals would fall, one after the other, over the cliff. They were then caught and slaughtered below. Buffalo found ideal conditions in the vast, rich grasslands of the great prairie. Numerous other animal species shared their way of life—antelopes, pronghorns, deer, bears, and all sorts of small animals and birds. There is evidence of a drought occurring during 1500 A.D. when many changes in life occurred. Some groups moved more eastwardly and hunting and gathering became a more common way of life than agriculture.

After Europeans arrived in the sixteenth century, many Native people adopted a mobile way of life. Buffalo provided the necessary materials for such items as skins and furs for tepee building and clothing, horns and

The most prominent and largest animal species of the Great Plains was the bison (bison americanus), today commonly called the buffalo. Considered an endangered species with only 1,000 remaining in 1900, it is now protected, with a herd of more than 30,000 living freely in national parks such as Wood Buffalo Park in Canada and Yellowstone National Park, in the United States.

Based on a photograph, 1860.

In the style of George Catlin, 1832.

Based on a photograph, 1860.

BLACKFEET

♦ Their name was given to them by Europeans for the color of their moccasins that were tinted black. In their own language they were known as the *siksika*.

♦ Language: Algonquian.

♦ Originally from Saskatchewan, they occupied the present-day regions of northern Montana and southern Alberta in Canada.

♦ They were subdivided into three groups, north to south: The Siksika, the Kainah (from *ahkainah*, "many chiefs," also called "Blood Indians" because of their facial paintings), and the Piegan (from *pikuni*, "dressed in poor clothes").

♦ Known as aggressive warriors throughout the region, the Blackfeet were a people organized into religious or warrior societies (such as the *ikunuhkahts*, "all comrades"). They divided themselves into small bands for hunting and reassembled at the end of each summer. The Gros Ventre were under their protection.

♦ In conflict with the Kootenay, the Flathead, and their Siouan neighbors (Crow and Assiniboin), the Blackfeet were also enemies of trappers. Their domination of the area declined after a smallpox epidemic in 1836.

♦ The population, estimated at 15,000 in 1780, is approximately 14,000 in Montana today, half of them living on the reservation.

The skill and bravery of the Plains people were put to the test during buffalo hunts. The hunters moved in small groups, hiding under prairie grasses, occasionally dressed in wolf hide held onto them with animal fat, as they approached prey. The buffalo, endowed with a subtle sense of smell but poor eyesight, were accustomed to coyotes and wolves, natural predators that killed the weak and sick, so they often tolerated the disguised hunters.

Hunting techniques included approaching buffalo as closely as possible in order to aim arrows with accuracy, but if the hunters came too close, they could set off a charge from a male buffalo. In this case, the hunter had to aim the arrow quickly and carefully. Hunters usually aimed at the hollow beneath the animal's shoulder to strike the animal's heart. In winter, the buffalo, like the moose in the Great Forest and in the Subarctic, became very vulnerable in the deep snow because of their weight. They were rarely able to escape hunters who were equipped with snowshoes.

Hunting season was year round for Native people, but the summer included collective hunts when animals were driven to a riverbed or a natural land depression. The Blackfeet used an ancient site in Alberta for their hunts as late as the middle of the nineteenth century. The strategy was planned with precision. The execution and the success of the enterprise depended upon the group efforts of all, for, if the herd was alerted, it would flee.

THE BLACKFEET AND GROS VENTRE

Based on a 1870 photograph.

GROS VENTRE

♦ They called themselves *haanin* or *aaninena*, "men of white clay." The tribe was related to the Arapaho who called them *hitunewa*, "beggars." The French called them the *Gros Ventre*, "big bellies."

♦ Language: Algonquian.

♦ Originally they came from present-day Manitoba and occupied the land from present-day northern Montana to the Missouri borders.

♦ They were primarily hunters.

♦ Like the Blackfeet, they were enemies of trappers, the Sioux, Crow, and Assiniboin, until 1867. They then allied themselves with the Crow against their Blackfeet protectors and were severely defeated.

♦ In 1780, they numbered 3,000. Today there are about 2,100 on the Fort Belknap Montana reservation, which they share with the Assiniboin.

To hunt beyond the limits of one's own tribal territory could spark a conflict. To avoid famine and replenish winter food resources, the people began their hunting season with certain dances and ceremonies—prayers and purification—to obtain the blessings and protection of animal spirits.

When Europeans arrived, the Plains people acquired two trade items that radically changed their way of hunting—horses and firearms. The horse made it possible to approach the herd quickly and without disguises. Pulling up alongside the buffalo, they could rapidly fire arrows, and guns were even more effective. Unfortunately, they were not the only hunters, and within a few decades, the immense wild herds of the Plains were decimated, mainly by American frontiersmen. ▲

Traditional buffalo hunting.

AROUND THE CHEYENNE

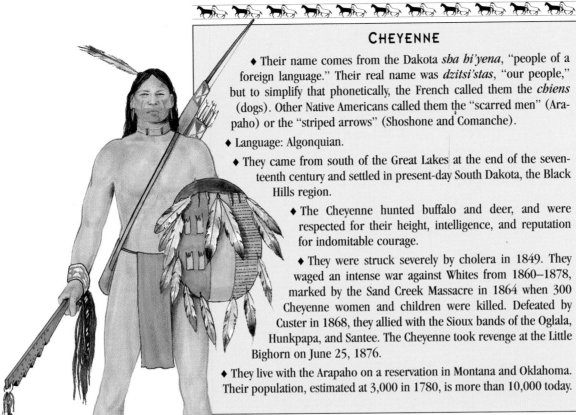

CHEYENNE

♦ Their name comes from the Dakota *sha hi'yena*, "people of a foreign language." Their real name was *dzitsi'stas*, "our people," but to simplify that phonetically, the French called them the *chiens* (dogs). Other Native Americans called them the "scarred men" (Arapaho) or the "striped arrows" (Shoshone and Comanche).

♦ Language: Algonquian.

♦ They came from south of the Great Lakes at the end of the seventeenth century and settled in present-day South Dakota, the Black Hills region.

♦ The Cheyenne hunted buffalo and deer, and were respected for their height, intelligence, and reputation for indomitable courage.

♦ They were struck severely by cholera in 1849. They waged an intense war against Whites from 1860–1878, marked by the Sand Creek Massacre in 1864 when 300 Cheyenne women and children were killed. Defeated by Custer in 1868, they allied with the Sioux bands of the Oglala, Hunkpapa, and Santee. The Cheyenne took revenge at the Little Bighorn on June 25, 1876.

♦ They live with the Arapaho on a reservation in Montana and Oklahoma. Their population, estimated at 3,000 in 1780, is more than 10,000 today.

Based on an anonymous etching, 1840.

The buffalo provided food and all the necessary materials for daily life for these hunting tribes. The male animal weighed more than a ton (909 kg), the females 1430 to 1760 pounds (650 to 800 kg). Their flesh was often prepared by drying, as a type of meat jerky. A common food of the Plains was *pemmican*, which was made with dried meat, reduced to powder, and mixed with fat, marrow, and berries. Often prepared in the form of sausages, using the buffalo's bladder or intestine, the pemmican lasted for years and was a particularly high-energy food supply.

Native people of the Plains successfully made use of nearly the entire animal:
• from the thickest part of the skin, such as the withers, they made shields. Clothes, moccasins, or blankets came from the finest part of the hide. Other leather was used to make tepee covers;
• from the bones, depending upon the shape and size, large digging tools, such as shovels, and smaller items, such as tomahawk handles, canoe rings (from the ribs), and containers (from the skull), and various small tools such as scrapers and awls were made;
• the largest bones were broken and their marrow extracted for the preparation of the pemmican. The smaller pieces were used as arrowheads;
• the headdress of the shamans or those of the bravest warriors were decorated with buffalo horns. Horns were also used for making bows or as storage pouches for ceremonial items, such as medicinal herbs.

Based on a photograph, end of nineteenth century.

Most of the animal was used. Each part filling a need, such as teeth (small tools), brain (skin softener), hooves (boiled and made into glue for hardening the shields), bladder (pemmican), intestines (bow strings), and tail (flyswatters). Even buffalo dung was used for fire fuel.

The prairie was a region with many other diverse types of game, including the Virginia deer and pronghorn antelope. The latter was as sensitive as it was quick, but the size of its herd, even larger than the huge buffalo herds, gave hunters the advantage. ▲

Algonquian tribes (from the Subarctic and Northeast forests), the Cree, and the Ojibwa occupied territories adjacent to the Plains. Bands of these tribes gradually adopted the way of life of the region, especially buffalo hunting. They are sometimes distinguished by the names, Plains Cree and Plains Ojibwa.

In the style of George Catlin, 1845.

PLAINS CREE

♦ This group was allied with the Assiniboin against the Siksika (Blackfeet) and the Dakota Sioux. Some joined their chiefs, Poundmaker and Big Bear, and the Assiniboin in the Burning Wood Revolt in 1885, which established a provisional government in Saskatchewan, Canada.

♦ Their population was estimated at 4,000 in the middle of the nineteenth century. Their descendants joined the Forest Cree on their reservation or intermarried with other tribes.

PLAINS OJIBWA

♦ Separated from their Great Forest brothers, the Chippewa (see p. 26), the Plains Ojibwa, also called the Bungee, allied with the Creek and Assiniboin from the beginning of the 18th century.

♦ Their numbers were estimated at 1,500 in 1850. Current figures are not available.

In the style of George Catlin, 1845.

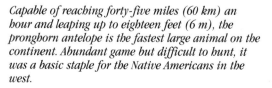

Based on an 1880 photograph

Capable of reaching forty-five miles (60 km) an hour and leaping up to eighteen feet (6 m), the pronghorn antelope is the fastest large animal on the continent. Abundant game but difficult to hunt, it was a basic staple for the Native Americans in the west.

ARAPAHO

♦ Their name is from the Pawnee, *tirapihu* or *carapihu,* "traders." They called themselves invna-ina, "our people." For their Cheyenne allies, they were *hitanwo'iv,* "men of the sky."

♦ Language: Algonquian.

♦ Probably migrating from present-day Manitoba, they crossed the Missouri and headed south through Wyoming, where they adopted the life of buffalo hunters.

♦ They fought against the Dakota, Kiowa, and Comanche alongside the Cheyenne, until a peace treaty was signed in 1840. They were then at war against the Shoshone, Ute, and Pawnee. The Arapaho joined the Cheyenne and the Sioux in struggles against the American troops until the Treaty of Medicine Lodge was signed in 1867, followed by their exile to Oklahoma.

♦ There were 3,000 at the end of the 18th century. Today there are from 5,000–7,000 on two reservations—one in Wyoming and the other with the Cheyenne in Oklahoma.

MASTERS OF THE PLAINS

Based on a photograph by W. Dinwiddie, 1896.

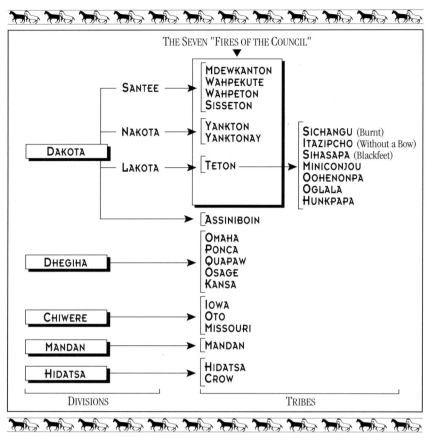

THE SEVEN "FIRES OF THE COUNCIL"

| DIVISIONS | | TRIBES |

While Algonquian-speaking people, along with the Blackfeet, dominated the northern part of the Great Plains, the Cheyenne and Arapaho dominated the western part and the Sioux occupied the center and eastern parts of the region. The attribution of the term "masters" of the Plains, was inaccurate, since it was often applied to only the Dakota Sioux who claimed preeminence. In fact, the Sioux (from the Ojibwa language, *nadowe-is-iw*, "enemies of the South") were not a tribe but a group of tribes who spoke the same language, Siouan, which some speculate had its origins from languages in the East, hence a possible link between the Siouan and Iroquoian languages. Of all the Sioux groups, the Dakota were those most often referred to in publications and media as maintaining dominance over their many Plains neighbors.

For the Sioux, war was waged after a number of preliminary ceremonies and in observance of the many taboos associated with warrior activities. Warriors departed for combat with the belief that they would not return, foreseeing their own death, but carrying with them objects that they believed conferred power and protection. Many warrior clans included shaman, whose role it was to assist and counsel. Shields were of great importance, not only for the object itself, but for the protective designs painted on it. Made from the buffalo's withers, where the flesh is thickest, and hardened by fire, the stretched leather shield was painted with ritual designs that appeared to the owner warrior during a vision. To complete the decoration, the shaman would provide the warrior with protective materials, such as feathers, scraps of fur, scalps, or small sacks.

The tomahawk was the warrior's most common weapon. Made of wood, bone, or horn, and decorated or sculpted, it was embedded with a round or pointed stone and utilized in close combat as a throwing weapon. The tomahawk was modified after contact with Whites. The round stone head was replaced by a strong metal axe and, in the eighteenth century, Native Americans adopted tomahawk models made in Europe that combined both the functions of war with peace, as they were designed to be both a hatchet and, with a hollow stem, a smoking pipe. The Sioux also liked "the crooked lance," a sort of large cane pointed at the end that was more a symbol of dignity than a combat weapon. Out of necessity, it was used at times to fight an enemy.

With the exception of tribes which belonged to the Siouan linguistic family but lived in other regions, the Winnebago in the Northeast, and Catawba or Yuchi in the Southeast, the Sioux Nation of the Plains was organized according to the chart above:

Note:
• The Wahpeton and Sisseton tribes are linked to the Santee division more for affinities that existed between them than for linguistic or geographic reasons.
• The Sihasapa, also called the Blackfeet, should not be confused with the Siksika (Algonquian Blackfeet).
• The Tetons alone comprised more than 60% of the Dakota Sioux nation.
Source: *Handbook of American Indians*, Smithsonian. ▲

DAKOTA SIOUX

♦ Their name means "Allies," in Santee Sioux. They were called *Nakota* in Yankton Sioux and *Lakota* in Teton Sioux.

♦ Language: Siouan.

♦ Chased by the Cree from the Mississippi springs region in the seventeenth century, by the beginning of the nineteenth century, the Dakota occupied a vast territory embracing most of present-day South Dakota and parts of North Dakota, Montana, Wyoming, Nebraska, Iowa, Wisconsin, and Minnesota.

♦ Until the middle of the nineteenth century, the Dakota had few clashes with Americans. Their primary occupation in the region was maintaining domination over their neighbors including the Ojibwa, Cree, Blackfeet, Crow, Pawnee, and Kiowa.

♦ In 1851, the Sioux boundaries were defined by treaty. In 1862, the Minnesota Santee were pushed from their best land and inadequately compensated. On the verge of starvation, they took advantage of the Civil War to attack Whites. The insurrection claimed 800 civilian and military victims and 80 Native Americans. The Santee were defeated at Woddlake on September 22, 1862. In 1863, the United States Army undertook a punitive campaign with the Whitestone and Badlands battles. The Sand Creek massacre brought the Cheyenne and the Arapaho into the war in 1865 in the battles of Platte Bridge and Wolf Creek.

The discovery of gold in Montana and in Idaho led to the opening of the Bozeman Trail, in violation of the treaties. This led to a new round of wars from 1865 to 1868, in which Red Cloud and Crazy Horse distinguished themselves. The Fort Rice Treaty in April of 1868 guaranteed some rights to Native Americans.

In 1872, the United States government began building a railroad between the Bighorn Mountains and Black Hills. War began again, marked by the Battle of Rosebud in 1876 and the defeat of General Custer at the Little Bighorn on June 25, 1876. After this disaster, the United States army tracked down the Sioux, who had taken refuge in Canada before returning to their reservation in 1881. In 1899, a Paiute named Wovoka announced the coming of a Native American messiah who would chase the invaders away. The Ghost Dance, reputed to hasten the event, spread throughout the Sioux tribes. This last large burst of resistance ended in the death of Sitting Bull and the massacre at Wounded Knee in 1890.

♦ The population of the Dakota Sioux was estimated at 25,000 in 1780. In 1970, they numbered 2,500 in Canada and 52,000 in the United States. Their reservations are located in Minnesota, Montana, Nebraska, and especially in North and South Dakota on the reservations of Pine Ridge, Rosebud, and Standing Rock.

Based on a photograph by F.B. Fishe, 1902.

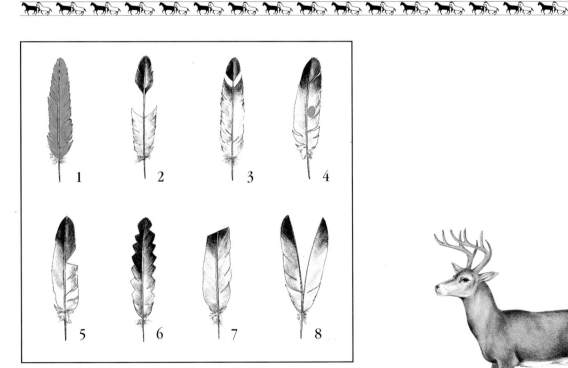

Beyond their decorative role, the number of feathers often signified a brave's war accomplishments.

1. *Wounded in combat.*
2. *Struck five blows at his enemies.*
3. *Wounded or killed his enemy.*
4. *Killed an enemy.*
5. *Killed an enemy and took his scalp.*
6. *Struck four blows at his enemies.*
7. *Slit an enemy's throat.*
8. *Wounded several times.*

The Virginia deer (odocoïleus virginianus) *is known throughout the United States as the white-tailed deer. It raises its tail to reveal a tuft of white hair that warns other deer of danger. Although less plentiful than the pronghorn, its range is much greater. Near extinction at the beginning of the century, the species is no longer endangered.*

WARRIORS OF THE CENTRAL PLAINS

Based on an early nineteenth-century drawing.

Dependent upon the buffalo hunt for survival, the Blackfeet, Cheyenne, and Dakota people followed the migration of the herds. Tepees could be erected in a few hours and quickly disassembled when it became necessary or urgent to move. Women were in charge of building the tepees and villages were preferred by the edge of rivers.

Clans, related tribal groups, acted in independent bands. They were composed of several families descending from the same ancestor from the female line. The clan leader would either be elected, according to acts of bravery, or designated by heredity. Tribes would often be comprised of three or four different clans, each having a leader, but the authority was often shared by several men, which encouraged a harmonious distribution of responsibilities and power.

Warrior societies played a particularly important role within Plains tribes. These political societies were ranked mainly by age among the Blackfeet, Arapaho, Mandan, and Hidatsa. Everyone, from the youth to the most honored warrior, could advance to different levels. Young men would enter into the hierarchy of the society by purchasing their rights from their immediate elders. This led to many gifts and festivities. The "buyer's" ambition moved him to a higher level within the hierarchy.

Non-ranked societies, competing within the same tribe, existed among the Teton Sioux, Crow, Cheyenne, Assiniboin, Omaha, and Ponca. There was no discrimination against those who joined their ranks, but the collective valor or the exploits of an exceptional warrior played a key role in ensuring the supremacy of a society. Also, there was fierce competition to attract the most valorous. Aggressive behavior was permissible.

A warrior's brave act, in certain warrior societies (the Teton's Miwa'tani or the celebrated Cheyenne Dog Soldiers), could include tying himself to a post with a large belt on the battlefield, which would force him into a situation where he would either conquer or die. The other tribal warriors did the opposite of what seemed to be most logical—they refused to join the battle if their brothers-in-arms were victorious, but fought with fury in the face of defeat.

These societies might also recruit women as combatants, such as with the Cheyenne, or for their skills in certain activities, such as the work accomplished with porcupine needles among the Cheyenne, Mandan, and Hidatsa. ▲

ASSINIBOIN

♦ Their name comes from the Ojibwa *usin-upwawa*, "he cooks using stones." The Dakota Sioux called them *hohe*, "rebels," and the French, "stone warriors."

♦ Language: Siouan.

♦ They came from the East and from Lake Winnipeg and Lake Nipigon, and settled in present-day southern Canada, along the Saskatchewan and Assiniboin rivers by the end of the eighteenth century.

♦ The Assiniboin were hospitable, hunting people who coveted the buffalo.

♦ A branch of the Yanktonay in the seventeenth century, they distanced themselves from the other Sioux tribes and allied themselves with the Cree against the Dakota. They constantly waged war against the Siksika. They were severely stricken by smallpox in 1836.

♦ They numbered 8,000 in 1829, 4,000 after the smallpox epidemic in 1836, and 2,800 in 1985, on reservations in Montana and Alberta.

In the style of George Catlin, 1831.

Teton Oglala, from a painting, 1875.

Depending on the tribe, tepees were built on three or four base poles, to which were added some twenty supporting posts. Opening to the east in order to better shelter the occupants from the major winds, they had an opening at the top to allow smoke to escape. The Council tent, set up at the beginning of the summer for the clans' meeting, might reach thirty-six feet (12 m) in diameter.

THE DHEGIHA SIOUX

In the style of George Catlin, 1834.

Comprising a group of tribes speaking Siouan languages and living in the central Plains, the Southern Plains people probably came from the Ohio River Valley around 1500 and included, in the North, the Omaha, Ponca, Osage, and Kansa tribes and, in the South, on the lower Arkansas River, the Quapaw tribe. These Native people were both hunters and agriculturalists, growing primarily corn.

Tattoos and facial and body painting were common marks of the Plains warriors and considered protective virtues. For the Plains warrior, it was also a way of intimidating his adversaries by showing the testimony of his bravery and his exploits. Often, the warrior's horse was also decorated to portray its attributes as well as the merits of its rider. In the traditional rituals of combat, a scalp could be taken from a dead or wounded enemy. It would be a sign of a courageous exploit, much like the theft of his enemy's horse. But warriors sought to deliver a final blow by touching the enemy with the end of a "coup stick," a pole bent at one end, often covered with fur and decorated with feathers. This blow was testimony to acts of bravery already accomplished. (But European bounties were offered to settlers for Native scalps and they were also taken by Whites.) Through trading, Whites provided pointed lances and metal arrows. Warriors used simple points, firmly secured, which could be recovered and reused for game hunting. By contrast, the weapons of war had barbed points, which came off upon impact and remained in the wound. The warriors also used hand weapons—bludgeons, clubs, hatchets, and tomahawks.

IOWA

BLACKFEET

PAWNEE

TETON

War Paintings, in the style of George Catlin and Karl Bodmer.

Based on a photograph, 1875.

PONCA

♦ The meaning of the name is unknown.

♦ Language: Siouan—Dhegiha

♦ They lived at the intersection of the Niobrara and Missouri Rivers in Nebraska.

♦ Descendants of the Omaha, they had a very similar way of life.

♦ They were conquered by their enemies, the Dakota Sioux, and relocated in 1877 to Oklahoma. A small group refused to leave the territory, part of which became a reservation in 1889.

♦ Their population was estimated at 800 in 1780. There were 401 Ponca in Nebraska in 1944, and 2,272 in Oklahoma in 1985.

Based on a photograph, 1870.

OMAHA

♦ Their name means "those who march against the wind."

♦ Language: Siouan—Dhegiha

♦ They lived northeast of Nebraska, on the west banks of the Missouri River.

♦ Their villages consisted of dwellings made of soil or bark that were supported by wooden frames. During buffalo hunting season, they lived in tepees, as did other prairie tribes.

♦ At war with the Dakota, they had no large-scale clashes with Whites. They sold their land in 1854, except for one parcel from an area taken from the Winnebago, which became their reservation.

♦ They numbered 2,800 in 1780; 1,300 in 1970.

In the style of George Catlin, 1832.

KANSA

♦ Their name is from a Kansa clan name. It may have been derived from terms meaning "people of the south wind."

♦ Language: Siouan—Dhegiha

♦ They lived in the eastern part of the state that bears their name.

♦ Their way of life was similar to other Southern Siouan-speaking people.

♦ They may have met Coronado as early as 1541. Marquette encountered them in 1673. Assigned to a reservation in Topeka, Kansas, in 1846, their land was seized, little by little, by the federal government. They were then removed to Oklahoma to a reservation area near the Osage.

♦ Their population was estimated at 3,000 in 1780. In 1985, 543 were counted in Oklahoma.

THE CHIEWERE SIOUX

Based on a photograph from
the Simonin mission, 1868.

OTO

♦ Their name is from *wat'ota*, translated as or more accurately "lascivious" or "inconstant." They called themselves *chewaerae*.

♦ Language: Siouan—Chiewere

♦ They settled in Nebraska, on the lower Platte.

♦ They were hunters and farmers.

♦ In their westward migration, they probably separated themselves from the Iowa, then from the Missouri. They were visited by Cavelier de la Salle in 1680. In 1854, they ceded their territory. When their reservation on the Big Blue River was sold in 1881, they left for Oklahoma, where they shared reservations with the Ponca, Pawnee, and Missouri.

♦ They numbered about 900 in 1780, and around 1,280 in 1985.

"Those who belong to this earth" make up the Southern Siouan tribes of the Iowa, Missouri, and Oto tribes. In the fifteenth century, they apparently formed, with other Southern Siouan groups and Winnebago, a large Nation to the north of the Great Lakes. They lived a mobile life while maintaining certain traditions with the Northeast, combining farming and buffalo hunting.

For more than five centuries, Indian people traversed the Plains. Among the tribes who came from the bordering regions, many different language families were represented, including Algonquian, Siouan, Shoshonean, Kiowan, Penutian, Athapaskan, among others. This great diversity of languages caused great difficulty in most communication. Sign language was used among all the tribes as a type of universal language, which encouraged trade and was a method of quick communication. Trappers, and later soldiers, familiarized themselves with this indispensable language in order to trade or to establish cordial and trustworthy relations.

Among one another, the tribes used a number of conventional signs. ▲

Sign Language

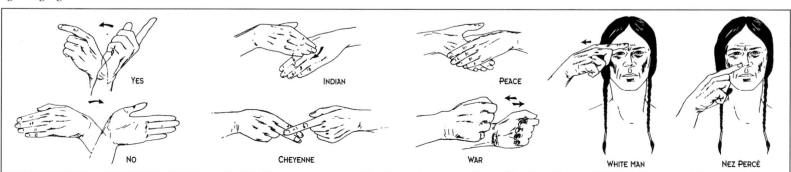

In the style of George Catlin, 1832.

MISSOURI

♦ Their name is possibly from an Algonquian word meaning "those who have pirogues." Another version offers "great muddy river," attributed to the Missouri River. They called themselves *niutachi*.

♦ Language: Siouan—Chiewere

♦ They lived in present-day Missouri, near the confluence of the Grand River and the Missouri River.

♦ They were farmers, cultivating corn, beans, and squash. They were also buffalo hunters.

♦ They were first encountered by Marquette in 1693. They suffered a major defeat by the Sac and Fox in 1798 and were conquered by the Osage at the beginning of the 19th century, before merging with the Iowa and Oto tribes.

♦ In 1780, their population was estimated at 1,000.

In the style of George Catlin, 1844.

IOWA

♦ Their name is from the Dakota Sioux language, *ayuhwa*, meaning "those who sleep." It could also come from *ai'yuwe*, meaning squash.

♦ Language: Siouan—Chiewere

♦ According to French merchants, the Iowa were very skillful traders and farmers. They measured their wealth in buffalo skins and in tomahawks, the bowls of which they sculpted from local rock.

♦ They encountered Marquette in 1674 and Lemoyne d'Iberville in 1702.

♦ They lived on a reservation in Kansas in 1836, some relocating to Oklahoma in 1883. They numbered 1,100 in 1760. Today, there are about 1,500 Iowa in Kansas, and more than 400 in Oklahoma.

Sign Language.

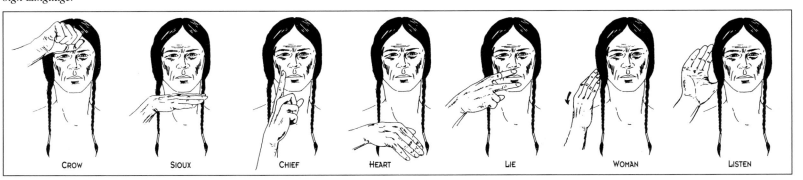

CROW   SIOUX   CHIEF   HEART   LIE   WOMAN   LISTEN

ALONG THE MISSOURI

In the style of Karl Bodmer, 1833.

Many Native people believed the world was inhabited by spirits to be feared, or beneficial ones to be honored. Thunder and lightning expressed the mood of these spirits. Cold and drought were the costs for the blessings of nature—the renewal of springtime, stream water, fruit on trees. Native Americans honored nature. If buffalo were plentiful on the Plains, it was believed spirits had granted the hunters' prayers. These spirits were invoked with devotion to keep the world in balance and the natural order of things, especially pertaining to food procurement, the hope that the hunt was fruitful, and the harvest abundant.

The people gave great significance to dreams and sought to achieve a state of mind that would lead to visions and hallucinations. The Mandan performed initiation rites at the time of the *Okipa*. Young men, after having been scarred on the back, shoulders, and legs, were suspended from the ridge pole of a ceremonial hut by wooden hooks that pierced their chest and arm muscles. Other rituals signified the corn harvest. Prolonged sweatbaths were common practice among Plains tribes, as they were in other regions. The baths took place in sweatlodges that were specially prepared for the occasion. Water was thrown onto stones placed on a fire, creating clouds of steam. Immobile, sweating, without food, the participant, near fainting, waited for the moment when he would begin to hallucinate. Important decisions for himself or the tribe—war, hunting, the migration of the village—were often based on the interpretation of these visions.

During adolescence, young men prepared to be hunters by withdrawing from the tribe for several days to fast. The first animal the hunter saw in his dream became his protector. He would never kill a member of that species but would always be inspired by it to make his "medicine." This medicine (derived from an Algonquian word, possibly the Chippewa, *mite-wiwin*) was a collection of small objects, a talisman that each warrior carried with him. It was indispensable, not as a cure as some have speculated, but as protection and to help find omens to guide him in decision making.

The shaman was believed to possess the power to communicate with spiritual forces that surrounded the tribe. He was an important figure, prestigious and influential—and sometimes feared—who often lived separately from the rest of the community, subjecting his body to diverse trials of purification, possibly even mutilations. The most important task of the shaman was to cure the sick.

Illness was often considered a punishment or a form of vengeance from malevolent spirits. To overcome pain was, therefore, a victory over these demons. For this purpose, the shaman had an assortment of objects and herbs at his disposal. Another of his responsibilities was to distinguish between good and bad omens sent by the spirits, omens that helped him make important decisions regarding the tribe's fate. ▲

MANDAN

♦ Their name is a distortion of the Dakota Sioux term, *mawatani*. They called themselves the *numakaki*, which means "the people."

♦ Language: Siouan.

♦ They inhabited present-day North Dakota, on the banks of the Missouri, at the confluence of the Little Missouri and Heart Rivers.

♦ They combined a life of corn farming and buffalo hunting, and were skilled potters. Centrally located on the Missouri, their villages became a trading center between the Northern and Southern tribes, and later, between the White merchants and other tribes for the fur trade. Organized into two half-tribes, the Mandan were closely linked to the Hidatsa and Arikara.

♦ They came from the Great Lakes area around the 1300s (probably a branch of the Winnebago) and were among the first Sioux to settle the Great Plains. La Vérendrye visited them in 1738, Lewis and Clark in 1804. Painters George Catlin and Karl Bodmer spent time with them in 1832 and 1833.

The 1837 smallpox epidemic struck them severely, leaving only 128 survivors (23 men, 40 women, and 65 children).

♦ They numbered 3,600 in 1780, 1,600 in 1837, before the epidemic, and 705 in 1970, living on the Fort Berthold reservation around Lake Sakakawea, North Dakota, with the Hidatsa and the Arikara.

HIDATSA

♦ Their name may be derived from "willows," the name of one of their villages. The Mandan called them *minitaris*, "those who crossed the water," referring to their first encounter on the banks of the Missouri. For the French trappers, they were the "River Big Bellies" (hence a possible confusion with the Gros Ventre).

♦ Language: Siouan.

♦ They were a branch of the Crow with whom they were closely linked.

♦ Neighbors of the Mandan on the Missouri, they had the same way of life. They did not practice the *okeepa*, but did the Sun Dance, which also features mutilation of the body. They had many societies to which both men and women belonged, including the Dog's Soldier Society for men and White Buffalo Society for women.

♦ They had the same "visitors" as the Mandan and were also stricken by a smallpox epidemic.

♦ They numbered 2,500 in 1780 and 731 in 1937, at Fort Berthold in North Dakota.

Communal shelter of the Mandan and Hidatsa.

In the style of Karl Bodmer, 1833.

Based on an 1840 painting.

Based on an early nineteenth-century etching.

CROW

♦ Their proper name was *absaroke*, "the bird people." The French called them "Crow People," from which their English name was derived.

♦ Language: Siouan.

♦ They settled in present-day Montana, along the Yellowstone River and its tributaries, the Bighorn, Rosebud, and Powder Rivers and, further to the south, along the Wind River in Wyoming.

♦ Separated from the Hidatsa around 1776, the Crow were a proud, belligerent people, with contempt for Whites. They subsisted on buffalo hunting. Their elegance earned them the name "the Brummels of the Native American world." At one time, they are recorded as having more than 10,000 horses.

♦ Lewis and Clark visited them in 1804. The Crow were in a permanent state of war with the Siksika and the Dakota. They served as scouts for the American cavalry.

♦ They numbered 4,000 in 1780. Nearly 8,700 were counted in tribal registers in 1992 on the reservation on the Bighorn River in Montana.

FARMERS OF THE PLAINS

ARIKARA

♦ Their name comes from the Pawnee, *ariki*, "horn," in reference to their headdresses. Their name for themselves was *tannish* or *sannish*, "the people." In sign language, the motions for their name were interpreted as "the corn eaters."

♦ Language: Caddoan.

♦ They lived on the banks of the Missouri between the Cheyenne River and Fort Berthold, North Dakota, near the Mandan and Hidatsa.

♦ Although they spoke a different language, the Arikara had the same way of life as the Mandan and Hidatsa, living in sod huts, in villages surrounded by palisades. They were corn farmers.

♦ At the end of the 18th century, they established good trading relations with the French. Lewis and Clark visited them in 1804. During their involvement in conflicts among fur traders, they found themselves on the emigrant route to the West. The Dakota and smallpox epidemics between 1837 and 1856 decimated them. In 1880, Arikara, Mandan, and Hidatsa were settled on the Fort Berthold reservation in North Dakota.

♦ They numbered 3,000 in 1780, 460 in 1970.

Caddo hut.

In the style of George Catlin, 1832.

Based on an early nineteenth-century print.

CADDO

♦ Their name is an abbreviation of *kadohadacho* (one of the tribes of the Caddo), meaning the "true chiefs." The Caddo called themselves *hasinai*, "our own culture."

♦ Language: Caddoan.

♦ They inhabited present-day southwest Arkansas and northeast Texas.

♦ They were farmers who also hunted buffalo.

♦ In 1541, the Caddo opposed explorer de Soto, who recognized their bravery, and in 1687, they encountered the survivors of la Salle's expedition. Lemoyne d'Iberville rallied them to the side of the French at the beginning of the 18th century. The Caddo first opposed the Choctaw, then allied themselves with the Choctaw against the Osage at the end of the 18th century. In 1835, they gave up their land to the United States government and settled in Texas. During the Civil War they remained loyal to the Union. They were moved to Kansas and finally settled on a reservation in Oklahoma with the Wichita in 1902.

♦ They numbered about 2,000 in the 18th century and 967 in 1937.

Native Americans made extensive use of tobacco combined with other plants (laurel, dogwood, red willow, poplar, and birch). They considered it an effective way to become closer to special spirits. Smoking the pipe was a ritual to be shared with friends and that facilitated thinking in a peaceful atmosphere. Passing the pipe around, from hand to hand, was a sign of great trust and was considered the best way to finalize a mutual agreement.

The Plains people maintained contact with spirits during many ceremonies using incantations and offerings, that elevated their state of consciousness. The Sun Dance is an example of this, in which they endured self-inflicted mutilations and other trials. Some believed that there was a hierarchy, according to the way they died—a warrior, for example, who was killed in combat, would not be close in the next world to a man who died of old age.

The death of a warrior triggered obvious manifestations of grief. A wife might beat her chest, cut her hair, and inflict severe wounds upon herself. Some tribes left the dead body in a cavern or on a tree, but most Plains people built a platform where the body would decompose slowly. Often, the favorite horses of the deceased were also killed in order to accompany their master to the next world. The warrior's weapons, tools, and goods were sometimes burned. ▲

In the style of George Catlin, 1834.

WICHITA

♦ According to sources, the name comes from *wits*, "men" or from the Choctaw *wiachitoh*, perhaps an allusion to their house, "great tree." They gave themselves the name *kirkitish*, probably meaning "the true people."

♦ Language: Caddoan.

♦ They lived in the Wichita Mountains in Oklahoma.

♦ They probably migrated from the South, raising corn, squash, and tobacco, which they traded with other tribes. They became buffalo hunters and were known to be honest and hospitable.

♦ The Wichita were in Kansas when Coronado encountered them in 1541. Their first treaty was in 1835 with the American federal government. They lived in Oklahoma until the beginning of the Civil War and then were moved to Kansas where they finally returned to the Caddo reservation in Oklahoma in 1867.

♦ They numbered 3,200 in 1780 and 460 in 1970.

Wichita shelter.

Sioux pipe in catlinite (a type of red clay) and wood.

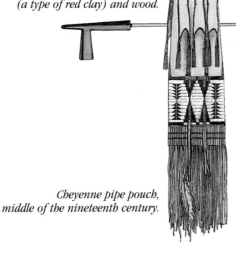

Cheyenne pipe pouch, middle of the nineteenth century.

In the style of George Catlin, 1832.

PAWNEE

♦ Their name comes from Paariki, "horned," an allusion to their hairstyles, or from Parisu, "hunter." They called themselves *chahiksichahiks*, "people."

♦ Language: Caddoan.

♦ They lived in the middle area of the Platte River in Nebraska.

♦ Divided into four tribes, the Pawnee were mobile, living in sod dwellings. Like the Mandans, they grew corn and hunted buffalo.

They had a complex religious organization where natural elements—wind, thunder, lightning, rain— were the messages from *tirana*, a superior spiritual force. During the corn-growing season, there were human sacrifices, usually female Comanche prisoners.

♦ The Pawnee were skilled in basket making, pottery and weaving.

♦ They migrated from the South and lived in the Plains area before the Sioux. Coronado encountered them in 1541. At the beginning of the 18th century, the Pawnee were allied with the French for trading and against Spanish expansion. Many were killed in the 19th century during combat with the Dakota Sioux. They supplied scouts to the U.S. Army. They yielded their territories by treaty and settled in Oklahoma.

♦ Numbering about 10,000 in 1870, 1,149 were counted in 1970.

In the style of George Catlin, 1832.

THE MAIN ROAD

In the style of George Catlin, 1834.

Based on a drawing from end of the nineteenth century.

COMANCHE

♦ According to some sources, their name came from the Spanish *camino ancho*, "main road," or from the Ute, *koh-maths*, "enemy." They called themselves *ne-me-ne* or *nimenim*, "the people."

♦ Language: Shoshonean.

♦ They were buffalo hunters, who lived in northwest Texas, and they were occasionally also engaged in farming. Famed as horsemen, they were known for their courage and their impetuousness, sense of honor, and conviction.

♦ They may have migrated from present-day western Wyoming, where they were linked with the Shoshone. They fought the Spanish and Apache before going to war with the Americans. Stronger because of their alliance with the Kiowa, their pillaging and killing multiplied at the beginning of the nineteenth century. After several violated treaties, the Comanche agreed in 1865 and 1867 treaties to withdraw to a reservation in Oklahoma, but they continued their raids until defeats in 1874–1875.

♦ They numbered approximately 7,000 in 1700, and 3,600 in 1985.

In the style of George Catlin, 1834.

KIOWA

♦ The original name is probably *ga-i-gwy* or *ka-i-gwy*, "dominating people."

♦ Language: Kiowan.

♦ In the middle of the eighteenth century, they occupied territory in present-day Oklahoma, Kansas, Colorado, New Mexico and Texas.

♦ They were buffalo hunters and were described as having a somber appearance and heavily built. The Kiowa kept an unusual biannual chronicle based on pictographs from 1832 to 1892, as did some Sioux.

♦ Before the eighteenth century, the Kiowa occupied a territory in Montana on the Yellowstone River, from which they created friendly bonds with the Crow. When horses were available, they migrated south and hunted buffalo.

In 1804, Lewis and Clark located them at the North Platte River. Upon reaching Oklahoma, they made an alliance with the Kiowa-Apache and their former enemies, the Comanche. Considered among the most aggressive of the Plains Indians, they were enemies of Whites.

♦ They numbered 2,000 in 1780 and 4,000 in 1985 in Oklahoma.

In the style of George Catlin, 1834.

In the first part of the nineteenth century, Whites agreed that the vast region in the center of the continent was inhospitable and unsuitable for colonization. That notion might have brought peace to the Plains Indians, had they not already paid a heavy price due to the European presence. From 1780 on, without interruption until the end of the nineteenth century, smallpox epidemics ravaged the tribes: Teton in 1780, Omaha in 1802, Comanche in 1815, Osage in 1828, Pawnee in 1831, Mandan in 1837, Crow in 1845, Iowa in 1848, Arikara in 1856, Kiowa, Cheyenne, and Arapaho in 1861, Assiniboin, Gros Ventre, and Blackfeet in 1871, to mention only the largest tribes. Several tribes lost nearly all their population, including the Mandan. Others lost most of their people. Diseases killed many more Native Americans than war.

At the same time, other events were taking place that hastened the decline of the Plains people, such as: the exodus of the Eastern tribes to Oklahoma, encroaching on the Osage, Kiowa, and Wichita territories; an influx of pioneers on the Oregon Trail beginning in 1843 or toward California after the discovery of gold in 1848; the Mormon migration in 1846; the development of communications from East to West—Pony-Express in 1860, Wells Fargo stage coaches in 1862, the construction of the "iron horse" transcontinental railroad from 1862–69; the accompanying destruction of the buffalo herds following the construction of the railroads; the growing number of

Sitting Bull, whose real name was Tatanka Yotanka, was born in 1831 or 1834, and was a Hunkpapa Sioux. He was a medicine man who became a warrior chief, fought against the Americans, and defeated Custer at Little Bighorn in 1876. He was killed on December 15, 1890.

Crazy Horse, whose real name was Tasunka Witko, was born in 1842 and was a renowned Oglala Sioux chief. He participated in the struggle against the Whites along with Red Cloud. He distinguished himself at Rosebud and Little Bighorn in 1876. He was killed shortly after his surrender on September 7, 1877 at the age of 35.

federal military installations...a long and tragic history that is beyond the contents of this book, and that found its epilogue at Wounded Knee in 1890, at the end of the so-called "Indian Wars." Indian battles that were won remain in the collective memory as witness to the Westward expansion—the Sand Creek Massacre and the battles of Washita, Rosebud, and Little Bighorn. ▲

THE SOUTHWEST

The Southwest includes the Mexican provinces of Sonora, Chihuahua, Coahuila, and, to the north, the states of Arizona, New Mexico, and southern Texas. Only the American territory will be examined in this work to conform to its designated subject area, North America.

The Southwest is a region of brilliant blue sky, a grand landscape of mountains, canyons, deserts, and truncated cliffs. The *mesas* are plateaus painted in warm clay colors of brown, ocher, red, and yellow, blended together. The mountainous peaks of the area are dotted with pine and juniper forests. To the south, in the desert, the sand and rock are filled with cacti and thorn bushes.

Occasionally in late summer, violent storms erupt, darkening the sky and transforming dry river beds, *arroyos*, into muddy torrents. The desert quickly changes and is filled with millions of tiny wildflowers that had been awaiting the rain.

The region was cold and humid during the Cochise period. The last retreat of the glaciers in the northern part of the continent modified a climate that became warm and dry, as it is today. Large game, such as the buffalo, moved north and hunters adapted to the new conditions and became farmers. Over time, the people of the area developed advanced agricultural techniques and arts. They may have been influenced by Meso-American civilizations in the South who had domesticated many local plants and became technically fine craftsmen in pottery, textiles, and jewelry. ▲

Nights are often cold, while some summer days are hot and oppressive. Birds, such as crested quails, mockingbirds, and shrikes, leave at dawn to feed, then take refuge in the shade the rest of the day. Peccaries and chipmunks brave the heat, but only a few lizards, like the chuckwalla, are capable of staying out in midday on burning rocks. Nighttime activity is more intense. Small rodents leave their ground holes to gather grain and some are attacked by predators such as snakes, birds of prey, and carnivorous mammals (badgers, foxes, coyotes).

The Kingsnake (lampropeltis pyromela) *can grow up to three feet (1 m) long. Harmless to humans, it feeds on small rodents.*

HOPI

♦ Their name for themselves, the word *Hopi* is also identified in two village translations as "good in every respect" and "is wise, knowing."

♦ Language: In early history identified as Shoshonean, but currently also accepted as from the Uto-Aztecan family.

♦ They were descendants of a wide diversity of tribes that slowly filtered into the area and began constructing homes from adobe and stone. They founded villages named Oraibi and Awatovi. Accomplished farmers and hunters of small game, the Hopi developed a rich and complex religious and cultural organization that supports the Kachina societies.

♦ The Hopi joined with other Pueblo peoples against Spanish domination in 1680 with the Pueblo Revolt. The Hopi also continually struggled against the Navajo, who surrounded them. In spite of the Spanish influence, they resisted Catholicism and remained devoted to their heritage and ancestral culture.

♦ Their number was estimated at 2,800 in 1680. Tribal registers list over 9,000 today.

In the style of E. Irving Couse, late nineteenth century.

Kachina dancer.

Three prehistoric cultures have been described by scientists as living in the region about 2,500 years ago. They are all identified as having descended probably from the Cochise population some 10,000 years ago. These are the Hohokam, Mogollon, and Anazasi people.

HOHOKAM

Settled in the Gila and Salt River Valleys in southwestern Arizona, these Native Americans were noted for their ability to make exceptional use of water resources. They developed a complex irrigation network for their fields. The ditches that carried the water were deep and coated with clay that limited evaporation and water lost through the ground. Small dams regulated the flow. This system allowed farmers to harvest two crops a year, one in the spring when the water was high due to the melting snow from nearby mountains, and the other at the end of the summer after monsoon rains. The Hohokam were skilled at making pottery, engraving shells, and carving stone sculpture. Perhaps as a result of drought, they abandoned many of their villages during the fifteenth century. The Pima and the Tohono O'odham in southern Arizona are probably descended from the Hohokam.

MOGOLLON

The Mogollon people lived along the mountainous area separating the Colorado Plateau region from the Sonoran Desert in central New Mexico and Arizona. Their dwellings were pithouses, located partially below the ground to adapt to temperature fluctuations. First hunters and gatherers, they later became skillful farmers, taking advantage of the nearby mountain streams to grow corn, sunflowers, squash, and beans. Proficient potters, the Mogollon were also expert jewelers, using different materials for their art—local turquoise, copper from Mexico, and shells from the Pacific Coast. They may

have migrated progressively northward, some joining their neighbors the Anasazi during the thirteenth and fourteenth centuries. It is possible some of the Zuni are descendants of the Mogollon people.

THE ANASAZI

The Anasazi occupied a vast region currently called the "four corners." It included the four present-day states of Utah, Colorado, Arizona, and New Mexico. First, hunters and gatherers, then farmers, they gradually became more stationary, setting up their wooden frame houses on the *mesas*. Eventually, they refined their building techniques and erected houses made from clay mortar and stone. At their apex in the thirteenth century, they built villages dug into the flanks of cliffs—Mesa Verde in Colorado, Canyon de Chelly in Arizona, and Chaco Canyon in New Mexico.

The men hunted, worked in the fields, or gathered in the *kiva* (subterranean round ceremonial house), probably to weave, talk, or participate in ceremonial activities. ▲

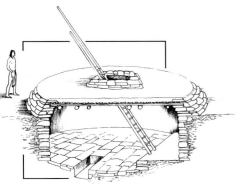

Round or rectangular, half or totally underground, a kiva is found in every Pueblo village. The spirits from the subterranean world are believed to enter through a hole in the top of the kiva. Kivas have two primary functions—as meeting or workplaces for men, and the ceremonial chamber for religious purposes. Women are admitted only during particular ceremonies.

ZUNI

♦ Their name is a Spanish derivation from the Keresan language, *si-ni* or *zuni*, whose meaning is unknown. They called themselves *a-siwi*, of unknown origin.

♦ Language: Zuni, possibly related to Aztec-Tanoan.

♦ They settled on the north bank of the Zuni River, tributary to the lower Colorado River, northwest of New Mexico.

♦ Farmers and expert potters, the Zuni practiced a form of *Kachina* religion similar to the Hopi. The society was organized on four levels. The priests were responsible for interceding with the powers above in order to bring fertility and life elements to the people.

♦ They took part in the 1680 Pueblo Revolt and at the end of the war settled on the present Zuni site in northwestern New Mexico.

♦ The Zuni numbered about 2,500 in 1680. Today their population is more than 7,700.

Based on a photograph, late nineteenth century.

PUEBLO

♦ The Spanish used this word, meaning in their language "town" or "village," to refer to Native Americans living in adobe (made of sun-dried clay bricks) and/or stone houses in small communities. There are twenty-two Pueblo villages, and linguists have identified four main Pueblo language families: Keresan, Zuni, Uto-Aztecan, and Kiowa-Tanoan. The Pueblo were primarily agriculturalists for centuries.

♦ The arrival of Francisco Vasquez de Coronado in 1540 was the beginning of Spanish interference throughout the Southwest. Spanish missionaries and soldiers settled the Pueblo region little by little and, at first, the Pueblo people tolerated them. In 1680, however, the Pueblo revolted against these intruders and some of their harsh tactics. At the end of the seventeenth century, the Spanish returned and took control of the villages.

♦ The majority of the Pueblo tribes live in northern New Mexico (Jemez, Santa Ana, Santo Domingo, Nambe, Zuni, etc.), but others, such as the Hopi, are in northern Arizona.

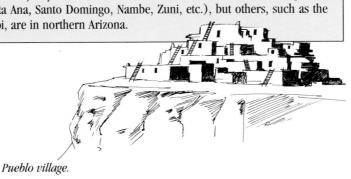

Pueblo village.

In the style of Joseph Sharp, 1893.

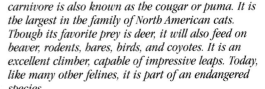

Called the mountain lion (felis concolor), this carnivore is also known as the cougar or puma. It is the largest in the family of North American cats. Though its favorite prey is deer, it will also feed on beaver, rodents, hares, birds, and coyotes. It is an excellent climber, capable of impressive leaps. Today, like many other felines, it is part of an endangered species.

THE MOUNTAIN REBELS

Geronimo, whose Apache name was Goyathlay, *"he who yawns," was born sometime between 1829 and 1834 in New Mexico. He was a medicine man who became a warrior and leader of the Chiricahua Apache and waged war against the Mexicans and Americans until 1886. He died in 1909.*

APACHE

♦ The Spanish probably borrowed the term from the Zuni language, *a-pacu*. There are several different groups of Apache tribes and some of the names they called themselves are *de-man*, *n-de*, and *haisndayin*, "the people."

♦ Language: Athapaskan.

  ♦ Apache people lived in Arizona, Colorado, and New Mexico.
    In the West—White Mountain, San Carlos, Cibecue, Tonto Apache.
    In the East—Chiricahua, Jicarilla, Lipan, and Mescalero Apache.

♦ The Apache constituted a heterogeneous group, each tribe differentiating itself by its geographic location and the influence of its neighbors. Thus, the Apache of the East were influenced in many ways by the Plains Indians. Known as formidable warriors, the art they developed to the highest degree of technical excellence was basketry.

♦ They migrated from the North, probably from Canada, perhaps as early as the tenth century, and had struggled against the Spaniards and Comanche since the seventeenth century. They also disrupted Pueblo life by raiding the villages.

After the annexation of New Mexico, a treaty was signed in 1852 between the Americans and the Apache, but hostilities resumed rapidly under chiefs such as Mangas Colorado and Cochise. The latter signed a treaty in 1872. After a short-lived truce, the Apache revolted again (1876–1886) with Victorio and Geronimo as chiefs.

♦ There are reservations in New Mexico, Arizona, and Oklahoma. Estimated at 5,000 in 1680, tribal lists show about 10,000 today.

Based on a late nineteenth-century photograph.

The reasons for abandoning cave-dwelling prehistoric sites remain a mystery. Something happened that upset the lives of the Hohokam, Mogollon, and Anasazi who coexisted in the region, causing their population to drop and forcing them to migrate, to break up communities, and perhaps to merge with other tribes. Were they victims of sudden climatic changes, drought, or heavy rainfall? Or were they threatened by the pillaging of other Indian groups? There are no answers to these questions. The Apache traveled and subsisted by hunting and gathering. They aggressively raided other Native settlements and may have contributed to the displacement of these tribes.

The Apache responded to the European onslaught with hostility, but the settlers were even more predatory than the Native warriors. The Apache were not the only victims of this implacable struggle; the Pueblo farmers also lost their freedom.

Western Apache, end of the nineteenth century.

Based on photographs of late nineteenth century.

Based on photographs of late nineteenth century.

The long and bloody history began one morning in May, 1539. A band of several hundred Native people gathered at the edge of the Zuni village to meet the first Spanish intruders. The Spanish "chief," who claimed to have the powers of a wizard, was called Estavanico.

These Europeans were the leading vanguard of an expedition sent by Antonio de Mendoza, viceroy of New Spain and led by Brother Marcos de Niza. Estavanico, arrogant and stubborn, approached the Zuni aggressively. He ended up riddled with arrows and caused the death of most of his escorts. The survivors fled and told their tale to Marcos de Niza. He approached the Zuni village carefully and saw, from a distance, a village that seemed to sparkle in the setting sun. On his return to Mexico, he gave the Spanish viceroy an impassioned description of a city covered with gold. The viceroy entrusted an important military expedition to Francisco Vasquez de Coronado. Seeking the legendary "seven cities of Cibola," Coronado's route was filled with destruction and massacres. For two years, he looked in vain for the rumored fabulous treasures across Arizona, New Mexico, and as far as Kansas—to no avail.

The failure of Coronado's expedition led the Spanish to change their strategy but not their brutality. They established three goals in order to conquer these lands—reduce Apache and Pueblo opposition, convert Indian people to Christianity, and control the lands and resources by protecting the area with *presidies,* or forts. The Spanish used the rivalries among the Native Americans to establish their dominance over the region, a method the French and English would profit by in other times and places. The policy was very successful but the Pueblos, whom they held nearly as slaves, revolted in 1680, and were temporarily successful. In 1694, however, the Spanish took control of the Pueblos again. ▲

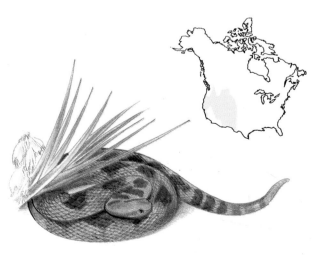

The Northern Pacific rattlesnake is a formidable predator. Growing to more than five feet (1.6 m) long, it feeds on small game and lizards.

57

In the style of B. Mollhausen, 1853.

ARIZONA FARMERS AND SHEEPHERDERS

NAVAJO

♦ The Spanish called the people, *Apaches de Nabajo*, from the Pueblo Tewa language, *navahu*, meaning "field" or "wide arroyo, valley," where there are cultivated fields. The Navajo call themselves *dine*, "the people."

♦ Language: Athapaskan.

♦ They settled in the northwest corner of New Mexico and northeastern Arizona.

♦ Less mobile than the other Athapaskan people, they farmed corn and fruit, and became proficient sheepherders. The Navajo developed and excelled at many different arts, including basketry, weaving, and silver work.

♦ Coming from the north, as their Apache relatives did, the Navajo lived closer to the Pueblo villages and were more influenced by Pueblo customs. They joined the Pueblo revolt in 1680. Ignoring the missionaries' work, they defended their territories. By 1850, three treaties had been signed by the Navajo and the United States government, but they failed to solve the conflicts. In 1863, Colonel Kit Carson, who was in charge of restoring order, massacred their flocks and imprisoned many Navajo. The Navajos were freed in 1867 and allowed to return to their land, where they finally made peace with their neighbors.

♦ Scattered throughout the large reservation (it takes up one-sixth of the state of Arizona and includes New Mexico and Utah), the Navajo, skillful and enterprising, have enriched their communities by raising sheep and benefiting from natural resource development on the land.

♦ Estimated at 8,000 in 1680, there are more than 160,000 today, the largest Native American population on the continent.

Navajo hogan. The wooden structure is covered with sod or bark.

From the middle of the seventeenth century, some Apache settled in villages that were similar to those of the Pueblo, where they combined farming and hunting and raising sheep and horses. The Apache and Navajo were opponents of the European and American invasion. Their struggle ended in the last years of the nineteenth century with confrontations led by Narbona, Ganado Mucho, and Manuelito for the Navajo, and by Mangas Colorado (Red Sleeves), Cochise, Victorio, and Geronimo for the Apache. The Navajo won the right to return to their land after several years of exile. The Apache were divided, some returning to Arizona and New Mexico, while others were sent to Oklahoma.

The Pima and Tohono O'odham (also known as the Papago) in the South and the Yuma of the far southwest of Arizona had less contact with the Spanish and, although not as eventful, their history was equally bloody. Defeated several times by the Spaniards, and later by the Americans, the farmers finally allied with the Americans against the Apache who consistently raided their villages.

Some Southwestern people, out of reach of the settler's grasp, had the good fortune not to come in contact with them until the eighteenth century. The first time the Yuman group, the Havasupai, encountered Europeans was in 1776, when Franciscan Francesco Garces came across them in a hollow in Cataract Canyon. The Havasupai, or "people of the blue-green water," were farmers and hunters, and are still there. ▲

Navajo shaman.

YUMAN

♦ Their name is a contraction by the Spaniards of the word *yahmayo*, "chief's son," the title of the person who will inherit the chief's power. They called themselves *kwichana*.

♦ Language: Yuman, related to the Hokan family of languages.

♦ The Yuman comprise a group of ten separate tribes (Walapai, Havasupai, Yavapai, Paipai, Mohave, Quechan, Maricopa, Diegueno, Cocopa, and Kiliwa), who live in areas of Arizona, California, and Baja Mexico.

♦ The Yuman were warriors, hunters, fishermen, and accomplished farmers, who used advanced methods of irrigation.

♦ Some Yuman met Hernando de Alarcón in 1540, but most were in contact with other Spanish traders and explorers from the very beginning of the eighteenth century. Some relinquished territory to the United States through the Guadalupe Hidalgo Treaty in 1848.

♦ About 3,000 in 1776, today about 6,500 live in Calif. and Ariz.

In the style of Arthur Scott, 1855.

Papago shelter.

Navajo weaving.

The roadrunner (grococcyx californianus) is a bird indigenous to the Southwest. When taken by surprise, it can run very quickly and suddenly change direction. These birds eat insects, lizards, scorpions, and small snakes.

CALIFORNIA
THE GREAT BASIN
THE PLATEAU

Because California, the Great Basin, and the Plateau are regions that seemed to share environmental, cultural, and historical features, they have been occasionally combined in the literature. An increase in research and knowledge of the diversity in these areas has led to their being considered separate regions.

CALIFORNIA

In many areas, California has the most consistent climate with moderate temperatures of all the states on the North American continent. The soil is fertile and well irrigated by a large river network. The exception is in the Mojave Desert in the south, which constitutes a more arid enclave near the Great Basin region. In California, the Indian population was large and enjoyed optimum living conditions, abundant game, and rich and diversified vegetation. All the material needed for the manufacturing of tools and weapons and the building of shelters was available.

This population shared a great similarity of customs and way of life, despite the great diversity of languages. More than one hundred languages were derived from the Athapaskan, Penutian, Hokan, and Yukian language families. The people lived in harmony with each other, exchanging their goods and respecting their neighbors' territory. Disputes between the tribes were often resolved by negotiations rather than by warfare.

THE GREAT BASIN

This region, which includes Nevada, Utah, and large parts of the states of Oregon, Idaho, Wyoming, and Colorado, is geographically separated into two areas.

1) The Great Basin is a vast plateau, more than 3,000 feet (1,000 m) high, bordered on the west by the Sierra Nevada range (Mount Whitney, over 12,000 feet [4,341 m]), on the north by the Snake River Valley and Salmon River mountains, on the east by the Teton and Wahsatch mountains, and on the south by Death Valley at the Mojave Desert border.

2) To the east is the Colorado Plateau, where the Green and Colorado Rivers are surrounded by mountain ranges with several peaks over 12,000 feet (4,000 m) high.

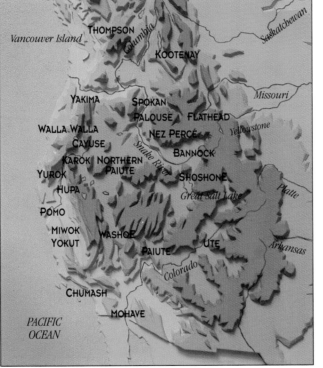

The Great Basin is one of the most arid regions in the world. The heat during summer is intense and much of the region consists of mainly desert, sand, and rocks. Infrequent but violent monsoons maintain the level of ponds, but more frequent irrigation comes from the mountains, whose brooks and streams feed small rivers.

THE PLATEAU

Bordered on the East by the Rockies, the Plateau includes southern British Columbia and a large part of Washington, Oregon, Montana, and Idaho. Several language families shared this region including the Algonquian, Athapaskan, and Penutian. Indian peoples include the Nez Percé, Cayuse, Yakima, Walla Walla, Klikitat, and the Salish groups—Coeur d'Alêne, Flathead, Shuswap, Coville, and others.

The life of the people was influenced by means of communication and trade. To the north, the Fraser, Bridge, and Lillooet Rivers, to the south, the Columbia and its many tributaries. These water routes were an inexhaustible reserve of food resources (salmon, sturgeon, trout) for the river tribes. The rivers also were the means of travel that furthered trade relations between the Pacific Coast and the interior, facilitating the exchange of goods and foods. ▲

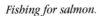

Fishing for salmon.

CALIFORNIA

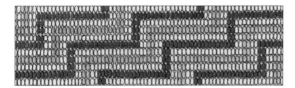

A t the border of the desert that now bears the native name, the Mohave lived along the lower part of the Colorado River. On small areas of fertile ground, they grew corn, beans, and squash, supplementing their diet by picking berries, figs, and roots, and also by catching fish and rabbits. Two characteristics distinguished the Mohave from other California tribes—a penchant for war toward their Yuman neighbors who lived downstream on the Colorado River, and their extensive trade network.

In southern California, other tribes, who also spoke the Hokan language, lived by the sea—the Tipaï, Luiseno, and Chumash. The Chumash were excellent fishermen, trapping whales, dolphins, seals, and sea otters. They traveled in simple wood boats called pirogues, which were protected with a tar coating. Three or four men could harpoon prey or catch fish in the mesh of their nets made of woven sea grass. In the low coastal waters, fishermen set fish traps or used toxic plants to immobilize the fish. They also harvested shellfish such as oysters, mussels, and scallops.

Further north, tribes whose language stemmed from Penutian (the Yokut, Miwok, Costanoan) spread out in villages in houses that were shaped like cones or domes with grass or wood coverings. The women were skilled at basketmaking. The tribes lived relatively peacefully under the guidance of the wealthiest member. This honor was often hereditary and could be assumed by a woman. ▲

In the style of H.B. Mollhausen, 1857.

MOHAVE

♦ Their name is from *hamakhava*, "three mountains."

♦ Language: Hokan.

♦ They lived on the banks of the Colorado River between the Needles and the entrance to the Black Canyon.

♦ They were farmers, but warriors were known for their athletic abilities.

♦ They first encountered the Spanish at the end of the 16th century. After skirmishes with Spanish and Americans, their territory became a reservation in 1865.

♦ Estimated at 3,000 in 1680, about 700 are on the reservation today.

With the exception of a few locations including southern Canada and the Ohio River Valley, the wapiti deer (cervis elaphus) can be found throughout North America. The most frequently hunted animal by Native Americans, its antlers provided the material for making spoons and many different types of tools.

MIWOK

- Their name means "men" in the Miwok language.
- Language: Penutian
- They inhabited present-day Yosemite Park, east of San Francisco.
- They were hunters and farmers.
- Forced to accept the presence of missionaries, they took part in several revolts. Some Miwok villages were ravaged by the Mexicans in 1843. The discovery of gold motivated miners needing labor to launch hostile expeditions against several tribes.
- They numbered about 11,000 in 1770. Only a few hundred remain today.

Miwok dwelling.

Dancer, in the style of W. H. Rolofson, 1856.

CHUMASH

- Etymology unknown. They were also called the Santa Barbara and Santa Rosa Indian people.
- Language: Hokan.
- They inhabited the southern coast of California and a few islands near Santa Barbara.
- Mainly subsisting from ocean resources, the Chumash were also skilled stone and wood-carvers. The women made fine baskets.
- They were visited by the Portuguese explorer Cabrillo in 1542. Five Franciscan missions were established in their territory from 1771 on. These new living conditions led to an Indian revolt in 1824.
- Numbered 2,000 around 1770, there are only a few Chumash living today.

YOKUT

- The name means "men" in their own language. They were also called *mariposans*.
- Language: related to Penutian.
- They inhabited the San Joaquin Valley.
- They were hunters and farmers.
- Many escaped the Spanish missions, but were victims of the American expansion during the Gold Rush of 1849.
- They numbered about 18,000 in 1770 and about 1,000 in 1930.

In the style of Léon de Cessac, 1878.

In the style of Léon de Cessac, 1877.

FISHERMEN AND BASKETMAKERS

Based on an etching, late nineteenth century.

POMO

♦ The name means "men" in their dialect. *Pomo* was also a suffix associated with the names of villages (Ballokaïpomo, Yokayapomo, etc.).

♦ Language: Hokan

♦ They inhabited the coastal region just north of San Francisco.

♦ They subsisted on acorns (a staple of their diet) as well as hunting and fishing. They were known for working with shells and meerschaum, a type of fine clay. The women made the most intricate baskets in California using a variety of techniques and materials.

♦ For the most part, they were little influenced by the Franciscan missions.

♦ Numbering 8,000 in 1770, today there are about 1,000.

Located in northern California, the Pomo have been considered three distinct groups because of their geographical differences. The largest group lived on the coast in a windswept area. The second group lived beyond the tall sequoia forests in the pleasant valley of the Russian River, and the third group inhabited the banks of Lake Clear (130 square miles [200 km²]), which provided an inexhaustible reserve of fish and a resting point for migratory water game. The different environments did not affect the cultural unity of the Pomo who had established a type of monetary system for trade with other tribes for fiber ropes, arrowheads, seal furs, and shells, among other items. One of the Pomo's sources of wealth was salt, which the brackish waters deposited in their areas during the summer. This prized staple was available to other Native Americans in exchange for gifts, but thievery was widespread.

Many of the Indian people of the region shared the same customs and traits—social structures based upon family, strong defense of their land, supremacy and authority granted to the wealthiest, generally peaceful living conditions—preferring negotiation to confrontation. Active trading networks existed between tribes. The Pomo of the coast traded with their neighbors inland, as well as the Yurok of the Klamath River and the Hupa of the Trinity River.

Ordered by military officers to convert the Native Americans to the "true faith," Franciscans and Dominicans founded twenty-one missions from 1769 to 1820, and from San Diego in 1769 to San Francisco in 1776. The combination of the sword and the cross led to the enslavement of many Native Americans. Forced to leave their villages, they were relocated to mission sites and became farmers. Their living conditions were harsh; three quarters of them died within a few dozen years, victims of epidemics, harsh treatment, overwork, and insufficient food.

California's independence from Mexico in 1823 marked the end of the Spanish mission system. The new political system focused on the appearance of American ranches. Native people were recruited to work, but the system turned out to be no better. The Gold Rush and the expansion of America hastened the decline of the large populations of Native Americans in California, despite several Indian revolts. ▲

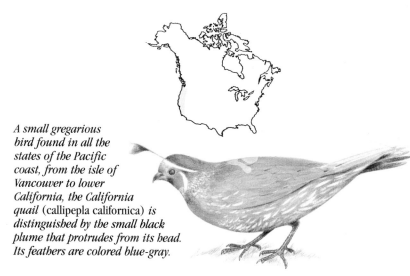

A small gregarious bird found in all the states of the Pacific coast, from the isle of Vancouver to lower California, the California quail (callipepla californica) *is distinguished by the small black plume that protrudes from its head. Its feathers are colored blue-gray.*

Based on an etching, around 1850.

YUROK

♦ Their name is from *yuruk*, a Karok term meaning "downstream."

♦ Language: related to the Algonquian.

♦ They lived near the lower Klamath River.

♦ They were gatherers and fishermen.

♦ The Yurok came into contact with Europeans comparatively late and experienced only minor conflicts with colonists and gold prospectors. Their territory was made into a reservation in 1855. Today, one band of the Yurok has a 228-acre (92 ha) reservation called the Resighini Rancheria in northern California.

♦ Estimated at about 2,500 in the nineteenth century, there were about 1,000 in 1985.

In the style of John Daggett, end of the nineteenth century.

In the style of Edward S. Curtis, beginning of the twentieth century.

KARUK

♦ Their name probably comes from the word *karuk*, meaning "upstream."

♦ Language: Hokan.

♦ They lived near the middle Klamath River.

♦ Hunters and fishermen, their history is similar to that of the Yurok.

♦ About 1,500 in 1700, there are about the same number listed in the tribal census today.

HUPA

♦ Their name is from the Yurok language and relates to their location, the "Hoopa Valley."

♦ Language: Athapaskan.

♦ They lived on the Trinity and Klamath River, and in the New River and Hoopa Valleys.

♦ Their villages contained small cedar dwellings spread out around sweatlodges (buildings that were heated by steam from water poured over hot stones). The women were skilled basket weavers and the men were expert woodcarvers. Based on individual wealth, the Hupa society was regulated by a complex social structure, but conflicts were usually resolved by compromise and with compensation.

♦ Isolated in the valleys, they came into contact with Europeans fairly late, around 1850. The American government established a reservation in 1864.

♦ About 1,000 in the mid-19th century, their population has grown to more than 4,000 today.

THE GREAT BASIN

With the exception of the Ute of the Colorado Plateau, the other tribes of the Great Basin—the Shoshone, Bannock, Paiute, Kawaiisu, and Washoe tribes—lived in areas sheltered by mountains and not influenced by other cultures. Their main activity was subsistence. They searched for and gathered resources and hunted in small family groups throughout the year, although larger groups worked together in times of abundance and during certain times of the year.

As a result of their rather mobile way of life, tribal political and social organization with most of the Great Basin people was simple. The family was the primary unit or groups of four or five families who would travel together. An elder often presided over specific ceremonies—hunting or war expeditions. Selected for his knowledge and courage, the elder's power ceased when the action was completed. Important group decisions were made after consultations with elders who were well known for their wisdom.

At the beginning of the nineteenth century, the Americans who came into contact with Native people of the Great Basin, called them "diggers" in reference to their food gathering, which included digging for roots, insects, caterpillars, snakes, lizards, and small rodents. Fortunately, nature sometimes provided other opportunities: at the end of winter, chipmunks would reappear in great numbers, as would water game—geese, ducks, and curlew, for whom the swamps and the ponds were resting places. The people used rush duck decoys to lure birds into traps and gather their eggs. They also harvested cattails and abundant catches of fish, dried and gutted, would be set aside for winter. Those located close to the Plains rode ponies to hunt buffalo.

When warm weather returned, the people moved toward higher, more comfortable altitudes. This move was repeated each year as lakes and streams were transformed into muddy marshes. In September, pine cones were harvested from large trees, thirty to thirty-five feet (10 to 12 m) in height, growing on the sides of the mountains among banks of juniper. Since the trees produced cones only once every two or so years, scouts were sent annually to find new trees. Once located, men, women, and children harvested pine cones and ate the seeds, one of the basic staples of their diet.

In the late fall, Native people returned to the desert, hunting for the desert hare, the celebrated blacktail. Although tracked throughout the year, the blacktail were especially abundant as winter approached. Long nets, 300 to 450 feet (100 to 150 m) in length, were made from hemp fiber. Several nets were placed in special areas in a valley and groups of people with noise beaters chased the animals toward the traps. ▲

Found throughout much of the North American continent, the coyote (canis latrans) is capable of running more than 300 miles (500 km) in one stretch. A predator that often competes with man, the coyote enjoyed the respect of the Native Americans of the Great Basin because it provided warning signals, such as alerting people to the danger of a cougar nearby.

Three plants were an important part of the diet of the Great Basin Native Americans.

A. The Cattail plant (typha latifolia) can reach a height of seven feet (2.5 m). The young shoot was eaten raw or made into a gruel, and the root dried and ground to make flour.

B. The Camas plant (camassia quamash) is a variety of lilac with delicate violet-blue flowers. Its bulb is also edible.

C. The Bitterroot (lewisia rediciwia), a small plant with white or light purple flowers, grows in forested areas. Its roots are edible.

BANNOCK

♦ The name is an English corruption of the Shoshone, *pannaitti*, the name used for themselves, *ni-mi*, "the people."

♦ Language: Shoshonean.

♦ They lived in southeast Idaho, later in the western region of Wyoming and southern Montana.

♦ From the beginning of the eighteenth century, the Bannock had ponies and hunted buffalo. They traveled in small bands, living in reed huts covered with grass mats in summer and in small, partially underground shelters in winter. Salmon was a favorite fish and women were skilled basket weavers.

♦ Proud and quick to take offense, their conflicts, first with the Black-feet and Nez Percé, then with Whites, were ongoing. They suffered from smallpox epidemics. Defeated by the U.S. Army on the Bear River (1863), they were assigned to the reservation at Fort Hall in Idaho (1868). They revolted in 1878 under the leadership of Buffalo Horn.

♦ Numbering 5,000 in 1829, there are about 3,500 Shoshone-Bannock in Idaho today.

Based on an 1880 document.

From an early nineteenth-century drawing.

SHOSHONE

♦ Their name is of uncertain origin, first recorded by Meriwether Lewis in 1805 as *sosonees*, or "snake people." Some other Native people referred to them as "grass-house people."

♦ Language: Shoshonean.

♦ The Shoshone were spread out over a large Great Basin area, including to the north—in eastern Idaho, western Wyoming, and northeastern Utah near the Great Salt Lake, as well as in the west—southern Idaho, southwest Utah, and northern Nevada.

♦ Like their eastern neighbors, they mainly subsisted on hunting the buffalo. As they obtained horses, they introduced them to neighboring tribes, such as the Blackfeet, Crow, and Nez Percé. The western Shoshone tribes were more sedentary, concentrating on food gathering and salmon fishing.

♦ In ongoing conflict with their Indian neighbors, the Shoshone remained neutral as much as possible with Europeans. They even provided scouts for the "blue coats," and obtained, in 1863, the two million acres of the magnificent Wind River reservation in Wyoming.

♦ Numbering about 4,500 in 1845, the Shoshone are about 5,000 in Wyoming today, although they share the reservation with some Arapahoe.

In the style of C.C. Nahl, 1866.

Around Colorado

The Paiute made distinctive cone-shaped baskets for gathering pine cones from the Nevada Singleleaf, or the Colorado pine, which grows mainly in Utah, Arizona, and New Mexico.

The appearance of the horse modified the Colorado Ute's way of life. As they obtained horses from their neighbors, the Plains tribes, from the seventeenth century on they moved onto the Plains to hunt bison. They were in contact with the Spanish because of conflicts with the Comanche, Apache, and Navajo, while other Native groups of the region remained isolated for a longer period of time. The other Native people did not encounter many outsiders until the arrival in 1847 of the Mormons, or "Latter-Day Saints," led by Brigham Young. Relations with these newcomers, who settled by the Great Salt Lake, deteriorated rapidly, giving rise to disorder and confrontations.

At the same time, another major event was occurring—the discovery of gold in California on January 24, 1848, at Captain John Sutter's sawmill. Within a few months, the news spread and a rabble of prospectors, down-and-outers, and adventurers beat their way to California and Nevada where gold and silver had also been discovered. The gold rush quickly upset the balance of population in the region, and greatly disrupted life for all inhabitants. Only a few prospectors discovered large veins of ore; for most the struggle was fruitless.

Some Native American populations were forced to either relocate or endure the introduction of diseases and epidemics. Cholera alone claimed more than 2,000 victims. In 1872, silver ore was found on Ute land, in the San Juan mountains. Prospectors and colonists waged a relentless campaign to remove the Utes from the region. Led by Chief Jack, the Ute revolted. In September, 1879, they inflicted heavy losses on the American cavalry at the Battle of Milk Creek, before being forced to surrender their weapons. ▲

Based on a photograph of 1860.

Paiute shelter.

PAIUTE

♦ Their name could mean "the true Ute."

♦ Language: Shoshonean.

♦ The northern branch of the Paiute lived in northern Nevada and in southeastern Oregon. The southern branch lived in southern Nevada and southeastern Utah.

♦ Organized into small autonomous bands, they lived in the nineteenth century almost as they did in precontact times.

♦ As gold seekers and colonists rushed to the West, it was the Mormons, not keen on this "invasion," who armed the Native Americans. The northern Paiute were granted reservations in 1865, the southern Paiute, a few decades later. They joined Bannock's Revolt in 1878.

♦ They numbered 5,000–6,000 in 1985 on the Nevada reservations of Duck Valley, Pyramid Lake, Walker River, and on California *rancherias*.

The black-tailed jackrabbit (lepus californicus) *is more similar to the hare than the rabbit. Plentiful in the American West, is distinguished from other species by a small tail with a white border.*

Based on a photograph from 1868.

In the style of Edmund O' Beamon, 1871.

UTE

♦ Their name and its variations (Uta, Utaw, Utsia, Youtah) were probably taken from the name of the state, Utah. "Utah" was an oral borrowing from the Spanish *yutas*. Utes call themselves, *nu-cl*, "Indian, person." The Lakota Sioux and the Cheyenne called the Ute, "black people."

♦ Language: Shoshonean.

♦ The eastern Ute lived in central and western Colorado; the western Ute in western Utah.

♦ Reputed to be aggressive, and allying with the Shoshone and Bannock, they reacted to the settlers' invasion by stealing cattle and horses. They subsisted mainly on hunting buffalo.

♦ Under Chief Ouray, their relations with Whites became progressively more peaceful, except for a revolt in 1879 called Milk Creek Battle.

♦ Numbering 4,500 in 1845, today the population is about 2,500 in Colorado.

WASHOE

♦ Their name is from the Washoe *wa-siw*, possibly meaning "people from here."

♦ Language: Hokan.

♦ They lived in western Nevada.

♦ They had exceptional basket-weaving skills.

♦ They were defeated by the Paiute, who pushed them toward the area of Reno (1862). Settlers took over allocated reservations before the Washoe arrived (1865).

♦ Numbered at 1,000 in 1845, the tribal lists total about 800 in Nevada today.

Based on a photograph from 1890.

Commonly called land squirrels or "Swiss squirrels," because of their striped fur, chipmunks are small animals that are fond of pine forests that provide them with hazelnuts, grains, fruits, and berries.

THE PLATEAU

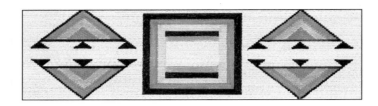

Traditionally, the Coastal Salish traded with interior tribes who spoke the same language, but their most active trading partners were the Chinook, a network of autonomous small tribes scattered along the lower Columbia River. The Chinook had two major activities: salmon fishing and trading. They dominated the trade in fur, dried fish, fish oil, shells, and baskets. They also traded slaves.

Trading activities went on near the juncture of the Columbia and Deschutes Rivers. Negotiations were conducted in a language that was a combination of Salish, Chinook and Nootka. Commonly called "Chinook," this jargon included French and English words dating from the beginning of the nineteenth century, when Whites took part in the activities. The presence of White traders was understandable because, since 1775, ships had been making stops along the coast and trading products made in Europe with Native people. Metal utensils had been used for many years.

Because of this trading center, the region was a mosaic of different people and cultures, influenced by each other. People from the Western Plateau had adopted traits of the people of the Pacific Coast. Others from the Eastern Plateau, (Kootenay, Coeur d'Alêne, Flathead, Nez Percé, Yakima, Cayuse) adopted the way of life of the Plains people, which was mainly focused on buffalo hunting.

People living in the central region who spoke Salish (Shuswap, Thompson, Lake, Sanpoil, Spokan) were less influenced by external forces. Their lives were regulated by the rhythm of the seasons and the constant need to obtain natural resources for the community. At the beginning of spring, both men and women scattered into the natural environment of the Plateau. Men hunted rabbits and caught fish while women gathered roots and edible plants. In April, winter camps were abandoned and the tribes settled along the river banks until late summer.

Fishing sites were carefully chosen for trapping or harpooning fish returning to their spawning grounds. To prepare a fishing site, fishermen hollowed and lined the narrowest passages with stones and white pebbles to help them see the furtive glitter of the salmon swimming upstream. In some areas, Native fishermen set up wooden dams to trap fish. They fished all through the summer until the end of the spawning season.

In the fall, the people of the Plateau returned to their subterranean dwellings that were covered with dried grasses and branches. Food and wood were carefully dried and stored. During the winter, people stayed close to camp. Women made baskets and clothing while men played games or made brief outings to hunt game. The winter solstice was an occasion for feasts and dances to appease spirits and wait for the return of spring. ▲

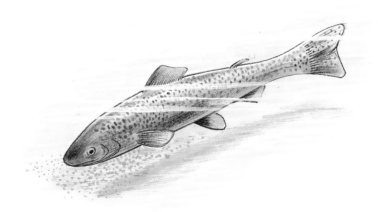

Several salmon species inhabit the rivers of the Pacific coast. The Chinook salmon (oncorhynchus tshawytscha) *is one of the most common species. It is very popular with fishermen, as are the sockeye salmon* (oncorhynchus nerka) *and the coho salmon* (oncorhynchus kitsutch).

SPOKAN

♦ Etymology uncertain; could translate to "people of the sun."

♦ Language: Salishan

♦ They lived in eastern Washington State.

♦ They were fishermen and hunters of all game, including buffalo.

♦ They resisted the American army for two years until the Fort Elliot Treaty was signed in 1855.

♦ They live on reservations in Montana and Washington. There were about 2,000 Spokan in 1780; 2,100 live in Washington State today on the Spokan Reservation.

In the style of Paul Kane, 1847.

In the style of James Teit, 1900.

THOMPSON

♦ Their name was given to them by Europeans, referring to the Thompson River. The people called themselves *ntlakyapamuk*, meaning unknown.

♦ Language: Salishan.

♦ They inhabited the Thompson and Fraser River valleys, British Columbia.

♦ They were fishermen and hunters of caribou, deer, moose.

♦ The Thompson were decimated by an onslaught of miners into their territory in 1858 and by smallpox epidemics in subsequent years.

♦ The Thompson still live on narrow pieces of land in this vicinity. There may have been as many as 5,000 in 1780; they numbered 1,776 in 1906.

IN THE HEART OF THE ROCKIES

Based on a late nineteenth-century photograph.

Driven from the continent by the last glaciation, horses returned to the New World with the Spanish on their ships. At the beginning, it appeared that Native Americans believed man and horse to be a single being, like the mythological centaurs of ancient Greece. The first Native Americans to acquire horses were the Comanche, who traded slaves to the Conquistadors for them. In 1680, a large number of horses escaped the Spaniards, who were at war with the Pueblo. Afterward, horses rapidly populated the prairie and greatly altered American Indian life.

During the eighteenth century, through trade and theft, most of the tribes living in the central Plains had integrated the horse into their way of life. This included the Navajo, Apache, and Ute, then the Osage, Kiowa, Cheyenne, and Arapaho, followed by the Pawnee, Crow, Shoshone, Dakota Sioux, and Mandan, and finally the Cree, Ojibwa, Blackfeet, and Nez Percé.

The century-long dispersal throughout the prairie transformed the small Andalusian horse, a descendant of fine and spirited Numidian and Arab breeds noted for speed and endurance, which had to face the rigors of winter and the attacks of wolves. Natural selection favored the strongest. The species lost several inches in its withers and gained a new name—mustang (from the Spanish *mestengos,* meaning "stray"). Around 1800, two million mustangs roamed freely in the central United States and were introduced to the Plateau region.

The Yakima controlled vast horse herds. The Nez Percé were known as superb breeders and trainers. The Cayuse (whose name would be adopted by the Whites to designate Indian ponies) raised *appaloosas,* which were widespread among the Native people living by the Palouse River. ▲

WALLA WALLA

♦ Their name means "small river."

♦ Language: Shahaptian/Penutian.

♦ They inhabited the lower Walla River (in the southeastern portion of Washington State and northeastern Oregon).

♦ Their traditional culture centered around fishing.

♦ They participated in the resistance struggles of the Plateau tribes against European oppression from 1853–1858.

♦ The Umatilla reservation in Oregon has a combined population of 1,000 (including Umatilla, Cayuse, and Walla Walla).

Based on a late nineteenth-century photograph.

PALOUSE

♦ Etymology and meaning unknown.

♦ Language: Shahaptian/Penutian.

♦ They lived along the Palouse River, in Washington State and Idaho.

♦ They hunted buffalo and were allies of the Nez Percé.

♦ With other Indian groups, they resisted White domination (1848 to 1858). They were the last to continue fighting. Included in the 1855 Treaty, they refused to live on a reservation.

♦ There were 1,600 in 1805, 82 in 1910.

THE CAYUSE

♦ The meaning of their name is unknown. Their own name for themselves was *wailetpu*.

♦ Language: Wailatpuan, a branch of the Shahaptian language.

♦ They lived in eastern Oregon.

♦ They hunted buffalo.

♦ They fought fiercely from 1847 to 1849 (Cayuse war) and from 1853 until 1856 in the Grande Ronde Battle in Oregon.

♦ They numbered 500 in 1780, 370 in 1937.

Based on a late
nineteenth-century photograph.

YAKIMA

♦ Their name means "fugitives." They called themselves *waptailmin*, "people of the narrow river."

♦ Language: Shahaptian/Penutian.

♦ They lived near the lower Yakima River, close to present-day Seattle.

♦ Hunters of buffalo, fishermen, and expert basket makers, they were friendly with the Nez Percé.

♦ Like their neighbors, they opposed the invasion of their territory and fought from 1853 to 1859 with their chief, Kanaïkin. Conquered, they submitted to the Fort Elliot Treaty and settled on a reservation in Washington State.

♦ Their number was 3,000 in 1780. The Yakima Reservation in Washington State is also home to other tribes, with a total population of 8,700.

Based on a late nineteenth-century photograph.

The royal eagle (aquila chrysaletos) *has a wingspan that can reach over seven feet (2.4 m). It lives in rocky summits and in flight, surveys the canyons in search of rabbits and small rodents. If its favorite prey is not available, it will feed on animal carcasses.*

73

FLATHEAD AND NEZ PERCÉ

If Europeans penetrated the Plateau fairly late during the historic period, their presence was already felt by the end of the eighteenth century through circulating trade goods among the Columbia Valley tribes and, unfortunately, through the spread of diseases. One story is that of the Sanpoil tribe, which was struck by an epidemic of smallpox in 1782 that killed nearly half of the community. Influenza, measles, and cholera also ravaged the tribes. In 1805, Lewis and Clark's expedition, guided by a Shoshone woman, Sacajewea, encountered the Nez Percé and the largest tribes of the Plateau. On their return, the explorers related the hospitality of the Native Americans living in that region. Trade relations developed to mutual satisfaction.

In the following years, an increasing number of immigrants traveled the Oregon Trail. They considered American Indians troublesome neighbors. The government negotiated a series of treaties with the tribes but the Yakima revolted in 1855. In 1860, gold was discovered on Nez Percé territory, which resulted in a gold rush. The Nez Percé had just one-eighth of the territory guaranteed by the previous 1855 treaty and the government pressured them to move. The tribe rebelled in 1877 under the leadership of Chief Joseph. Conquered the following year, they later surrendered, with 418 survivors, of whom 87 were warriors. Deported to Oklahoma, 103 more died of malaria. When the government authorized their return to the Northwest in 1885, through the intervention of General Miles who had conquered them, there were no more than 257 Nez Percé surrounding Chief Joseph— all that was left of a tribe that numbered 3,300 ten years earlier. ▲

In the style of George Catlin, 1832.

His true name was Hinmaton Yalatkit, (Thunder-that-comes-from-the-waters-beyond-the-mountains). Chief Joseph (1840–1904) received his nickname from the missionary Spalding. A perceptive and courageous war chief, he led the Nez Percé in their final revolt. The nobleness of his bearing commanded respect from his enemies.

NEZ PERCÉ

♦ Their name was used by the French to designate tribes whose members decorated their nose with a shell. Later, this name was used for a single tribe. They called themselves *nimipiu*, "the people."

♦ Language: Shahaptian/Penutian.

♦ They inhabited a large part of Idaho and northeastern Oregon (Snake and Clearwater Valleys).

♦ They were primarily buffalo hunters.

♦ Although peaceful, they opposed the actions of trappers between 1830 and 1840. They gave up a large part of their territory in the Walla Walla Treaty in 1855, but their reservation was invaded by gold prospectors in 1860. After the 1863 treaty, they retained only the Lapwaï reservation. By 1877, the decision to open the Wallowa Valley to gold prospectors triggered a revolt led by Chief Joseph. The rebellion ended tragically in 1878.

♦ They numbered 4,000 in 1780. Two centuries later, 3,000 are counted in the tribal census in Idaho.

An object of great worship by the Native Americans, the black bear (ursus americanus) *was also hunted for its fur, which was used as ornament by the chiefs and shamans. Bear fat made a mosquito repellent paste and its claws were talismans considered to be endowed with spiritual powers.*

KOOTENAY

♦ This is a mispronunciation of their name, *kutonaga*, by their Blackfeet enemies. The Nez Percé and the Salish called them "watermen."

♦ Language: Unknown.

♦ They lived in southeastern British Columbia, northwestern Montana, and northeastern Washington.

♦ They were buffalo hunters.

♦ The Blackfeet were their enemies; their relations with Whites were cordial.

♦ Numbered at 1,200 in 1780, today they live on reservations, part in Canada—549 in 1967, and part in Idaho—123 in 1985.

In the style of James Teit, late nineteenth century.

SALISH OR FLATHEAD

♦ The Salish tribe is sometimes called the Flathead, a term used by Whites to describe tribes that deformed young children's skulls by pressure to their foreheads as infants. The term was first recorded in use by the Chinook and was adopted by Canadian trappers. The Salish did not practice this type of infant mutilation.

♦ Language: Salishan.

♦ They lived in western Montana and along the southern areas of the Northwest Coast of Canada. This section refers to the inland Salish.

♦ They were buffalo and deer hunters.

♦ Driven west by the Blackfeet, the Flathead lived peacefully with American settlers. They gave up their territory to the U.S. government in 1855 for a reservation in Montana.

♦ They numbered 600 in the early 20th century. The Flathead reservation, also home to the Kootenay, and Pend d'Oreilles, numbers 6,700 today.

Based on an 1884 photograph.

The bighorn or Rocky Mountain goat (ovis canadensis) *is a social animal, an excellent climber, and a good swimmer. In the summer, lambs and ewes make up herds of about one dozen. In the winter, they descend into valleys with rams. It is then that the species is most vulnerable to predators such as wolves, coyotes, bears, and lynx. During the summer season, the royal eagle is also a threat on steep slopes.*

75

THE NORTHWEST COAST

About 150 miles (200 km) wide, the Northwest Coast stretches a lengthy 1,500 miles (2,300 km) from south to north, from the present borders of Oregon and Washington to Yakutat Bay in Alaska. Small in land area when compared to the Plains region or the Subarctic, this region has many of the most dynamic, bold, and mysterious Native cultures in all of North America—not unlike their environment.

It is highly probable that tribes who lived on this coast, such as those who spoke the Salishan or Penutian languages, first followed the same Bering Strait migratory route as other Native peoples—through the northern Canadian regions, then down into the valleys of the rivers rushing toward the Pacific. But where did the others, whose languages and cultures were unique, migrate from? One hypothesis is that maritime tribes came from the northern Alaskan coast or possibly even from Japan or Kamtchatka, through the Kuril Islands and the Aleutians, carried by ocean currents that followed the land mass. But this is only a hypothesis, for which there is no supporting evidence. Artifacts that provide clues are rare in this humid environment. The traces found prove a human presence only as early as 10,000 years B.C.

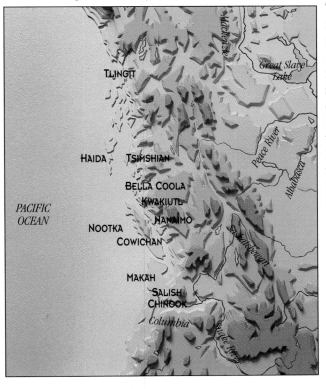

who were fed and housed. After the welcoming ceremonies, feasts, and dances, the potlatch ended with another distribution of gifts and speeches by the guests who presented gifts to their host.

The guests often organized a *potlatch* in return to demonstrate their own greatness and wealth. Such a feast required months (even years) of preparation by the organizer's relatives, his clan's members, and the slaves attached to their service—slaves who could find themselves among the gifts on the list along with canoes, sealskins, or barrels of whale oil. This value system, which closely linked the recognition of a person's rank with his capacity to distribute his riches, helped maintain an economic balance between all the tribes of the region. ▲

The people of this area created a hierarchical society of complex social and political organization. Roles were inherited and led to higher rank, as did wealth. Wealth was proof of hard work, skill, or fighting ability. It was granted to those who earned it and, in this culture, it was considered an honor to give it away. The redistribution of goods and wealth was carried out during the *potlatch* ceremony, common to most tribes of the region. Potlatches were organized for important events, such as moving into a new dwelling, attaining a higher rank or burial, a marriage, or a special birth. Dignitaries from other clans were invited to witness performances and the great generosity of the host that affirmed the superiority of the giver's clan. A potlatch often lasted several days and brought together hundreds of guests

A sea mammal, the orca (orcinus orca), is also called the killer whale. It can reach twenty seven feet (9 m) in length and has a voracious appetite, devouring fish, octopus, and sea birds. The orca's image is frequently found on the distinctively carved totem poles of the Northwest Coast.

MASTER SCULPTORS

Based on a nineteenth-century etching.

Carved in the trunks of thuja, or red cedar trees, the Haida's sea canoes could be as long as 54 feet (18 m) and seat more than fifty men.

HAIDA

♦ Their name is from *ha-te* or *ha-de*, the word for themselves, "the people."

♦ Isolated language, Haida. There are both southern and northern dialects.

♦ They settled on Queen Charlotte Islands in British Columbia and a portion of the Alexander Archipelago in southeastern Alaska.

♦ They were fishermen and remarkable wood carvers, skillful traders, and feared warriors.

♦ Explorers who visited them include Juan Perez (1774), Bodega (1775), and La Pérouse (1786). The Haida contracted smallpox during this time period.

♦ Numbered around 8,000 in 1760, there were more than 1,700 in 1984.

Generally made from the trunk of a thuja tree, the totem (from the Algonquian ototeman, *"he is one of my kin") tells the story of a family or a clan and features the animal protector associated with them.*

From the north down to Vancouver Island, the coast was indented and craggy because of the contours of the mountains. A dense forest covered the hillside to the edge of the sea, where Native Americans built their villages. The Northwest Coast people obtained food from the sea, and the necessary materials for building and crafts from the surrounding forests.

The fishing season began in the spring and ended in September. The sea was filled with herring, tuna, and smelt. Many species of sea mammals such as seals, otters, sea lions, and dolphins were also hunted. A beached whale provided enough food for the village for a long time. The Nootka and Makahs ventured through the high sea to hunt the whales. On the seashore, Native people harvested shellfish (mussels and clams) and sea bird eggs.

In late spring, the rivers were filled with the annual run of salmon going upstream toward their spawning area. The salmon harvest occupied men and women during the summer, when they left their villages and settled by the riverside. Like the Plateau, Aleut, or Alaska tribes, the people living on the coast used every means possible to snare their prey, including harpoons, nets, and dams. Ceremonies often greeted the first catch as many groups believed their dead were reincarnated in salmon to nourish the living and ceremonies were meant to encourage the salmon to return the following year. Women cleaned the fish and dried them on racks. In the fall, they fished for cod. Fall was also the time when Native people turned to the forest to hunt. In spite of the density of the forest and the difficult terrain, their efforts were rewarded by abundant game, including mountain goats, deer, elk, and bear, and all kinds of furred animals such as beaver, otter, marten, marmot, muskrat, and squirrels. ▲

Several Haida families lived in these large plank houses built from logs and sheared wood boards.

TSIMSHIAN

♦ Their name, *'cmsyan* means "inside the Skeena River." It is their name for themselves.

♦ Language: Tsimshian.

♦ They lived on an estuary of the Skeena River.

♦ They were fishermen especially of salmon, and hunters of bear and deer. They were closely allied with the Haida and Tlingit. Skilled wood, bone, and ivory carvers, they were well known for their sculptures.

♦ They had only rare contacts with the American world until the founding of the Hudson Bay Company in 1831. They yielded to pressure from gold seekers and other prospectors.

♦ They numbered 5,000 in the early twentieth century, with 9,400 in 1980.

Based on a late nineteenth-century photograph.

This stone axe was used in combat by the Kwakiutl. It was also used to execute rebellious slaves.

Masked Hamatsa dancer.

KWAKIUTL

♦ Renowned anthropologist Franz Boas typified the spelling and name in the late 19th century and wrote it as *kw'agu/l*, the meaning of which is unknown.

♦ Language: Wakashan (second division with the Bella Bella).

♦ They lived on the banks of Queen Charlotte Strait and its inlets.

♦ They were skilled navigators, fishermen, and hunters, as well as talented sculptors and good traders.

♦ After Bodega's visit in 1775, they became familiar with English and American explorers and traders. They managed to preserve their culture in spite of the arrival of missionaries.

♦ Numbering about 4,500 in 1780, there are more than 3,500 currently living on and off reservations.

TLINGIT

♦ Their name is derived from the Tlingit name for themselves, *li-ngit*, "human beings."

♦ Language: Tlingit.

♦ They inhabited the islands of the Alexander Archipelago at the farthest reaches of Alaska.

♦ They were salmon fishermen, sculptors, basket weavers, active traders, and formidable warriors.

♦ Their first contact was with the Russians. After the Chirikov expedition (1741), the Russians set up an outpost in the Baranov Islands and maintained strained relations with the Tlingit. There was a smallpox epidemic in 1837. Thirty years later, the Russians yielded Alaska and the Tlingit coast to the United States.

♦ The population has been stable, with 10,000 in 1750 and about the same in 1985.

Tlingit baskets.

In the style of Mikhail Tikanov, 1818.

In the style of Mikhail Tikanov, 1818.

These men were also formidable warriors. Their warrior activities, prefaced by long rituals, were launched to avenge any offense and resulted in war casualties and systematic pillage of the belongings of the conquered.

From fall to spring, when potlatch was not being organized, their time was spent planning war, engaging in artistic activities, or trading. The trade network lay between the coast and the interior. To the south, the Chinook were in contact with the people of the Plateau, but most of the products of the coast passed through the Tlingit villages. They were skillful traders who knew how to profit from all transactions, perhaps as a result of their being located in the far north, in between the Alaskan tribal trade and the Athapaskan trade to the East. They were actually the middlemen. The products of the coast included shellfish, bones, and whale oil, which were exchanged for caribou skins and copper from inland.

Tlingit families were matrilineal—as were most of the other coastal tribes—which resulted in a complex network of female responsibilities. Fathers were responsible for the education of their sister's children while their own children depended on the authority of the wife's relatives, such as the wife's brother. Knowledge was passed along orally and, from a very young age, children learned from their elders the clan's history and stories of warriors' exploits and accomplishments.

Youths were strictly disciplined, and young boys and girls were expected to be virgins until marriage. The passage from childhood to womanhood was marked by rigorous and restrictive rites. Some tribes observed individual fasting for several days, sitting, immobile, in a special small hut on the edge of the village, and rubbing their lips and faces with a hard stone for hours a day. The violation of these rites could mean bad luck for the rest of a young girl's life. The conclusion of this rite resulted in the placement of a labret, an ornament of wood or bone, through her lower lip.

Marriage was less a matter of love than a means of increasing the clan's wealth. The marriage ceremony was marked by several gift offerings. ▲

Whale fishing.

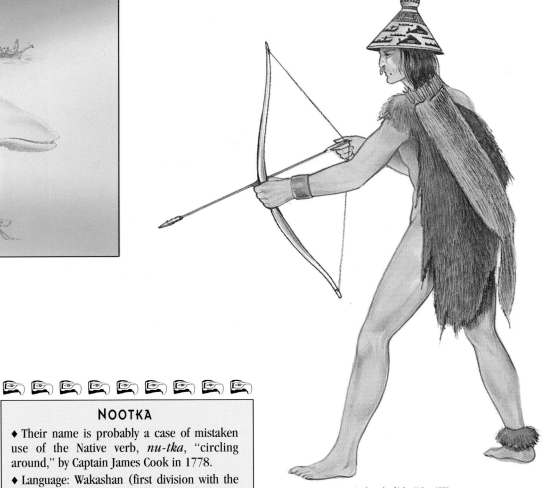

In the style of John Weber, 1778.

In the style of Jose Cardero, 1791.

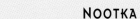

NOOTKA

♦ Their name is probably a case of mistaken use of the Native verb, *nu-tka*, "circling around," by Captain James Cook in 1778.

♦ Language: Wakashan (first division with the Makah).

♦ They inhabited the western coast of Vancouver Island.

♦ They were great hunters of sea mammals, such as whales, seals, and dolphins.

♦ Explorers included Juan de Fuca (1592), followed by Perez (1774), James Cook (1778), and Vancouver (1792). The founding of Victoria in 1843 marked the end of their cultural independence. Many converted to Catholicism.

♦ They numbered 6,000 in 1780, and 3,200 in 1967, increasing to more than 4,700 in 1984.

MAKAH

♦ The name from *ma'qa-a*, from the Clallam tribe. The Makah word for themselves is *q-idicca-atx*, "residents of the *q-idicca-atx*" or Cape Flattery area.

♦ Language: Wakashan.

♦ They first inhabited Cape Flattery (American-Canadian border), near Vancouver Island.

♦ They survived by gathering food and fishing, as well as hunting whales and seals.

♦ They gave up their territory to the United States government in 1855 but were granted a small reservation on the land itself in 1893.

♦ Numbering 2,000 in 1780, over 1,000 live at Neah Bay.

An inhabitant of the Rocky Mountains, from Alaska to Wyoming, the grizzly bear (ursus horribilis) may be as tall as six feet (2 m) when it stands up on its hindlegs. This omnivore subsists on various plants, fruit, mushrooms, insects, mammals, and animal carcasses. Great lovers of fish, grizzlies catch salmon with dexterity. They avoid humans but may be dangerous because they are unpredictable.

FROM PROFITABLE TRADES

CHINOOK

♦ The name is from *tsinuk*, a name given to them by their neighbors the Chehali. They were also known as *Flatheads* because they practiced the deforming of their children's heads.

♦ Language: Chinookan. Should not be confused with Chinook, a business language used in this area in the nineteenth century to facilitate trade.

♦ They inhabited the area from Willapa Bay to Tillamook Head, along the banks of the Columbia River, near present-day Seattle.

♦ They were fishermen and were active in the trade between tribes as well as between tribes and Whites. They captured and maintained Indian slaves.

♦ The Englishman John Meares, searching for furs, met them in 1788; the Lewis and Clark expedition in 1805. They were decimated by smallpox in 1829. Their survivors were progressively absorbed by other tribes like the Chehali, Salish, and Tillamook. No current population figures are available.

Based on an anonymous etching, circa 1880.

Native people living on the coast accumulated riches to gain respect by giving them away. This rite included men or women shamans with power as important as that of the chief of the tribe. They were feared for their frightening, ceremonial appearance in masked attire and the powers they were known to possess. Shaman treated illness and predicted the future.

In the North, the shaman rituals were exercised only in the presence of those who sought them out. In the South, especially among the Kwakiutl, the shamans' power manifested itself through powerful societies and dramatic portrayals. Initiates into these societies were drawn primarily from members of the tribe, who could pay for the shaman's services. The initiation ceremonies impressed and reinforced the power of the elite on shamans and the rest of the members of the tribe.

Native people of the Northwest Coast came in contact with the European world late during the historic period. The first encounters were in the eighteenth century as Russians arrived in the Bering expedition on the *St. Peter* and the *St. Paul*. A storm separated the two boats and the *St. Paul*, commanded by Captain Alexis Chirikov, reached an unknown coast, Chickagof Island, at fifty-eight degrees northern latitude. They found traces of a human presence and thought they had seen canoes. Some sailors sent to explore the area never returned.

In 1773, King Charles III of Spain, having learned of the Russians' misfortunes, ordered a flotilla placed under the command of Juan Perez to take possession of all the land. When they reached Queen Charlotte Island, the Spanish encountered the Haidas, who surprised them with their trading skills. In 1778, James Cook, on his third journey through the Pacific, encountered the Nootka on Vancouver Island. The Indian people were eager to acquire objects made of iron, especially knives and tools, from him. The Europeans wanted furs. The exchange could have been profitable to both parties if the greed of some of the Europeans had not offended some Natives who were accustomed to the subtleties of inter-tribal trading. Relations rapidly deteriorated during the following years. The French navigator La Pérouse, who explored the Tlingit coast in 1786, reported that the Native people's aggressive attitude may have been tempered by their fear of their firearms. ▲

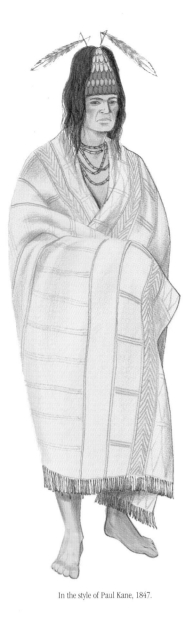

Bella Coola sun mask.

SALISH TRIBES

♦ Many groups speaking the Salish language occupied the islands and coasts of the region: Penntlatch, Comox, Homalco, Klahoose, Sliammon, Sechelt, Clallam, Halkomelem, Squamish, Nooksack, and Northern Straits people.

♦ The most numerous and influential were the central coastal Salish (Squamish, Halkomelem, Nooksack, Northern Straits people, and Clallam) who lived in southeastern Vancouver Island.

In the style of Jose Cardero, 1792.

The sea otter (enhydra lutris) *swims at great speed, remaining underwater for four or five minutes. It feeds on shellfish, crabs, sea urchins, and small fish. It makes a bed of algae to sleep on and takes refuge on land in case of danger from killer whales, sharks, or storms.*

Based on an 1868 photograph.

83

THE SUBARCTIC

The Subarctic region covers the largest portion of Canada and Alaska. This immense space has changed since the middle of the nineteenth century under the pressure of modernization, but it has not been subjected to the radical transformations that have affected the eastern and central United States, such as an increase in demographic makeup, heavy industrialization, and rapid deforestation. European immigrants preferred to move westward rather than head north of the Great Lakes where winters are severe. The Subarctic can be divided into three geographical areas:

1) A very mountainous region encompassing Alaska, Yukon, and British Columbia, located at the northern end of the Rockies and dominated by the imposing St. Elias range, of which Mount McKinley (18,200 feet [6,194 m]) is the highest peak. Large glaciers feed the rivers, which are filled with salmon. At middle and low altitudes, the region is thickly covered with vegetation and is home to diverse fauna from the deer family, including moose and caribou, as well as mountain goats, mountain sheep, and various types of bears.

2) The tundra, bordered on the north by the Arctic coast and including the territories of present-day northwestern Canada and the northernmost portion of Labrador. Isolated from the Pacific by a massive coastal range, these territories receive little precipitation. Even during the eight month winter, the coat of snow is rarely over twelve inches (30 cm) but the ground is frozen to a depth of 900 feet (300 m) with the permafrost. The spring thaw permits the growth of vegetation dominated by lichens that attract numerous migratory birds.

3) Farther south, the taiga, a vast pine and birch forest that stretches from the Atlantic to the Rockies. It includes a large part of Quebec, Ontario, Manitoba, and Alberta. Having a milder climate, the taiga is home to many animals including beavers, muskrats, foxes, moose, caribou, deer, wolves, and black bears.

With some variations depending upon the latitude, these three regions share a continental climate of great severity, with important differences in temperature. Summer is short and warm; winter is endless, with temperatures dropping to minus 22 degrees Fahrenheit (−30°C).

Native Americans of two linguistic families shared the Subarctic region. To the east were the Algonquian-speakers (Naskapi, Montagnais, Ojibwa, Cree) and to the west and north, Athapaskan (those of the northern language division called *tinneh* or *déné,* and the Chipewyan, Yellowknife, Dogrib, Beaver, Kaska, Tahlta, Carrier, Kutchin, Tutchone, Koyukon, Tanana, and others). The tundra Athapaskan, who inhabited the coldest regions, had the poorest natural resources and traveled in small groups of one or two families. Of peaceful disposition, they were primarily concerned with subsistence from one area to another. The Algonquian, who lived primarily in the forested areas, had a milder climate. They moved seasonally and many aggressively protected their hunting territories. ▲

An American version of the European reindeer, the caribou (rangifer taraudus) *is a congenial animal that often migrates in large herds of several thousand. In winter, lichens from the tundra are its basic food, and during the summer, it eats grasses, rush, and birch and willow twigs.*

HUNTERS OF THE GREAT NORTH

One common thread united most people of the region—the caribou. Like the buffalo for the Plains Indians, it provided meat, skins, and various resources that included bones, antlers, and tendons for weapons and tools. Native American life often followed the caribou. The animals moved north during the warm seasons for the birth of the young calves and returned to the forests when the cold season began.

From summer camp to winter camp, the people of the North never remained at the same place for long. Summer shelters were simple tepees covered with skin that could be set up and taken down quickly. Men hunted, fished, and built canoes while women tended the fires, water, cooking, and, when the hunters returned, cut up the hunted animals, drying the meat, tanning the skin, and making clothing. During seasonal migrations, women carried many of the loads. In spite of these many tasks, women often went unrecognized, eating after men and only if there was something left over. This state of subordination was common with tribes that lived under very harsh conditions—the need for a provider made the role of the hunter predominant. In winter, following the trails of animals they hunted, the Chipewyan made their camps further south in the forest. ▲

In the style of Alexander Murray, 1847.

KUTCHIN

♦ Derived from a misunderstanding of Kutchin names. The Kutchin name for themselves is *gw-icin*, "the people."

♦ Language: Athapaskan.

♦ Their region includes the upper Yukon valley, the Yukon Territory, and to the far east, the mouth of the MacKenzie River.

♦ They were hospitable, despite a reputation for aggression toward other Athapaskan groups. They were hunters and trappers of fur-bearing animals.

♦ The Kutchin were a group of eight or nine tribes, each having their territory—Arctic Red River Kutchin, Peel River Indians, Upper Porcupine River Kutchin, Crow Flats Kutchin, Black River Kutchin, Yukon Flats Kutchin, Birch Creek Kutchin, Chandalar Kutchin, and Dinhai Kutchin.

♦ Alexander Mackenzie met them in 1789. Their relationship with Whites was established afterward through the Hudson Bay Company. The discovery of gold in the Klondike Valley disrupted their nomadic life and freedom.

♦ They numbered 1,200 in 1936.

The spruce grouse (dendragapus canadensis) *inhabited the Subarctic taiga and tundra. The ruffled grouse* (bonasas umbellus) *shared the same environment.*

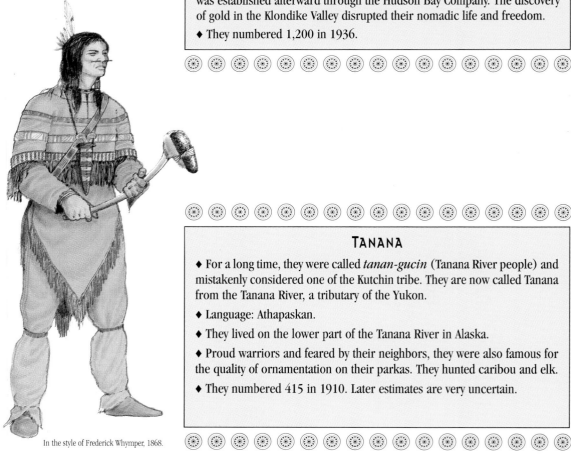

In the style of Frederick Whymper, 1868.

TANANA

♦ For a long time, they were called *tanan-gucin* (Tanana River people) and mistakenly considered one of the Kutchin tribe. They are now called Tanana from the Tanana River, a tributary of the Yukon.

♦ Language: Athapaskan.

♦ They lived on the lower part of the Tanana River in Alaska.

♦ Proud warriors and feared by their neighbors, they were also famous for the quality of ornamentation on their parkas. They hunted caribou and elk.

♦ They numbered 415 in 1910. Later estimates are very uncertain.

In the style of Émile Petitot, 1860.

DOGRIB

♦ Their name, *atimospikay*, was of European derivation meaning "dog side." According to legend, this tribe was born from the union of a woman and supernatural being that was half-dog, half-man.

♦ Language: Athapaskan.

♦ They inhabited the territory separating the Great Bear Lake and the Great Slave Lake.

♦ They lived in harmony with their neighbors, such as the Slave tribe. Tall and taciturn, they hunted caribou and musk ox.

♦ Pushed further north by the Cree incursion, they ceased to participate in the fur trade for fear of crossing into rival territories.

♦ They numbered 1,250 in 1670, and 1,700 in 1970.

YELLOWKNIFE

♦ Their true Chipewyan name *talzahotine* meant "Yellowknife," which referred to the color of oxidized copper. It was also translated as meaning "copper people."

♦ Language: Athapaskan.

♦ They inhabited the north and east banks of the Great Slave Lake.

♦ They were caribou and musk ox hunters.

♦ The history of the Talzahotine cannot be separated from their use of copper. Thanks to this metal, they could make weapons and tools, and enjoy a privileged position among tribes, but when the Europeans introduced iron and steel items to the market, the Yellowknife unable to compete, slowly migrated south.

♦ They numbered around 200 during the nineteenth century.

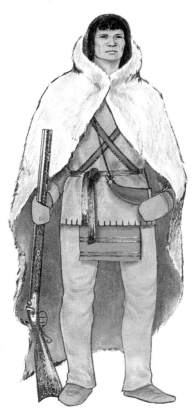

In the style of Robert Wood, 1821.

CHIPEWYAN

♦ Their name comes from the Algonquian Cree *ci-pwaya-n*, meaning "those who have pointed skins or hides," in reference to the pointed trim on their Athapaskan tunics.

♦ Language: Athapaskan.

♦ Their territory bordered the Great Slave Lake to the northwest, the Athabasca River to the southwest, and Hudson Bay in the east.

♦ They were caribou hunters and fishermen. Emile Petitot, a Catholic missionary, credited them with the same qualities as their neighbors—"innocent and natural in their lives and manners, a great common sense and a taste for justice."

♦ Ancestral adversaries of the Algonquian Cree, the Chipewyan had to surrender to them when the expanding fur trade brought Whites into their territory in 1717. The Chipewyan were pushed further north and west until a smallpox epidemic broke out in 1779, which severely struck both tribes.

♦ Numbering 3,500 in the early 18th century, 4,643 were counted in the 1970 census.

In the style of Émile Petitot 1862.

FROM MANITOBA TO LABRADOR

In the style of Peter Rindisbacker, 1821.

CREE

♦ Their name is derived from an obscure band of Indian people who roamed the region south of James Bay in the seventeenth century. The term is Ojibwa in origin and probably is a form of *kiristino* (Christian). By 1780, English traders had adopted the shortened form of Cree.

♦ Language: Algonquian.

♦ The Cree were the Native people bridged between the Algonquian and the Athapaskan. Split into four groups—the East Main Cree, West Main Cree, Tête de Boule, and Western Woods Cree, who lived on the land between the west bank of James Bay and Lake Athabasca. The Tête de Boule, a band of roaming hunters, lived in Quebec.

♦ Hunters and fishermen, the Wood Cree were known for their excellent handling of their birch bark canoes.

♦ The Cree settled in a strategic spot, and were at the heart of the French-English competition for the control of the fur trade. Allied with the Chippewa, they maintained good relations with Whites, at the expense of the Athapaskan of the North and West.

♦ Numbered at 15,000 in 1776, their population was severely decimated by smallpox and fell to 2,500 in the nineteenth century. There are about 10,000 today in Manitoba, and 5,000 in the Northern Territories.

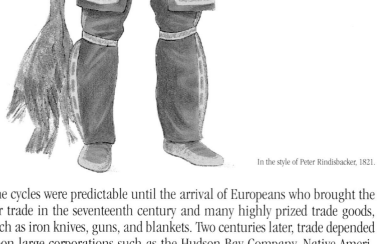

In the style of Peter Rindisbacker, 1821.

The Athapaskan of northern Canada and Alaska braved extreme cold, with temperatures dropping as low as minus seventy-seven degrees Fahrenheit (–60° C). Their subterranean dwellings were insulated with two layers of skins in order to insure better protection. The Algonquian-speaking people shared the same hardships but their environment offered a greater variety of game, such as beaver, porcupine, duck, and geese. The larger animals, caribou and elk, did not live in this area because they could not move well through the high, deep snows as compared to the stronger frozen tundra.

Spring was a time of deliverance. Native people were able to resume their traditional activities. The Naskapi went trout fishing, the Kutchin and Koyukon hunted muskrat, and many Algonquian-speaking people made maple syrup. Spring was also the time for tribal reunions and trading. Items available for exchange included flint, furs, copper objects (knives, awls), and dried foods. The Athapaskan-speaking people from the West began salmon fishing and all the tribes resumed the tasks of following caribou herds migrating from south to north across the vast spaces. The Chipewyan hunters again traveled the tundra, wearing caribou horns around their waists so that the banging of the horns might attract some solitary male who would follow, thinking there was a female to gain in combat with another male. The Naspaki women smoked meat and fish, and the Ojibwa harvested wild rice on the edge of Lake Superior.

The cycles were predictable until the arrival of Europeans who brought the fur trade in the seventeenth century and many highly prized trade goods, such as iron knives, guns, and blankets. Two centuries later, trade depended upon large corporations such as the Hudson Bay Company. Native Americans would then trade items in the outposts that were scattered throughout the region. They bought guns, powder, knives, and axes. The prices were based on the sole currency in use—beaver fur, the most prized fur in Europe for centuries. ▲

The wolf (canus lupus) was found throughout the entire North American continent. Gregarious and intelligent animals, they ran in packs of five to seven. Although in competition with Indian hunters, the wolf was held in high regard by most of the Athapaskan, especially the Chipewyan, who considered the wolf in the same category as the dog—a brother of humans.

In the style of David Pelletier, 1613.

NASKAPI

♦ Their name was given to them by the Montagnais as a derogatory term meaning "those who have no religion."

♦ Language: Algonquian.

♦ They inhabited the northcentral area of the Labrador peninsula.

♦ They were caribou and small game hunters.

♦ Allied with their Montagnais neighbors, their main enemies were the Inuit who lived north.

♦ There are a few hundred Naskapi who live today in Quebec.

In order to lure migratory birds to rest, thus exposing themselves to arrows or traps, Native Americans made decoys of wood.

Based on a nineteenth-century etching.

MONTAGNAIS

♦ Their name came from the French because of the topography of their territory. It refers to the "mountaineers." They called themselves *tshe-tsi-uetin*, "people of the north-north east."

♦ Language: Algonquian.

♦ They lived in southern Labrador, between the St. Lawrence Estuary and James Bay.

♦ They were fishermen and hunters and traveled in bands of fifty to one hundred.

♦ They were linked to the Naskapi and Cree by a similarity in language. Their traditional enemies were the Micmac and, especially, the Iroquois. Most converted to Christianity and became trusted trade and war partners of the French. The scarcity of fur-bearing animals and the presence of famine, war, and epidemics threatened them with extinction.

♦ They live on nine reservations in Quebec.

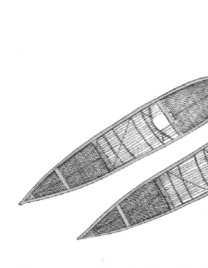

The snowshoes of the Kutchin and their neighbors were very narrow and could be more than two feet (75 cm) long. The Algonquian preferred ovalshaped shoes that allowed hunters to move more rapidly on the snow, a major advantage in locating large game.

THE ARCTIC

More than any other Native group, the Inuit probably resemble the first people who arrived across the Bering Strait into northern North America, perhaps from northeastern Siberia, near the North Pole. They slowly traveled east to present-day Alaska, traversing through ice floes or water routes up to the northernmost part of Canada and Greenland. They were probably the last to come from Asia into North America, around 3000 B.C. The Inuit, meaning "person, people" (from the western part of Greenland), were known to their southern neighbors as the Eskimos (from *esquimawes*, found in a 1584 English treaty to refer to people living at "graunde bay").

Three Inuit regions are identified, stretching more than 12,000 miles (7,000 km) east to west:

1) To the west, the whole Alaskan coast, from the Aleutian Islands to the mouth of the Mackenzie River. The southernmost Aleuts built their houses of wood and the bones of cetaceans, sea mammals. The northernmost lived in subterranean dwellings covered with sod.

2) Farthest east is Greenland. The Inuit lived there in stone dwellings and hunted whales in the Davis Strait. They were in contact with Vikings as early as the tenth century. From this relationship grew a successful trade in skin, fur, and ivory between Greenland and northern Europe.

3) The central region, from the Mackenzie River to the northern banks of Labrador, comprising the islands and territories around the northern part of Hudson Bay. In this region, the Inuit encountered the rigors of a hostile environment and led an incessant struggle for survival in the immense ice fields swept by polar winds. The elderly who could not keep up were abandoned with some supplies in an ice shelter or igloo. If they were short on food, they resorted to cannibalism. A child, generally a girl, was sacrificed, for boys were considered future hunters. Nothing could compromise the survival of the community.

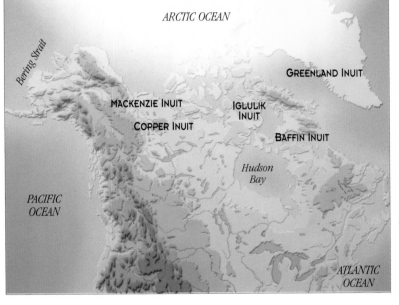

ARCTIC OCEAN

Bering Strait

GREENLAND INUIT

MACKENZIE INUIT

IGLULIK INUIT

COPPER INUIT

BAFFIN INUIT

Hudson Bay

PACIFIC OCEAN

ATLANTIC OCEAN

The difficult living conditions were reflected in their relationship with nature and the supernatural. The Inuit believed that the souls of men and animals transformed from one life to another, from one species to another. A complex ensemble of rituals surrounded these beliefs. For example, hunting and fishing activities were often separated, and the people would use different weapons and wear different garments during each of these activities. They ate caribou and seal meat on different days. Trapped animals were killed and their souls were given thanks for the success granted the hunter. Satisfied with the homage that it had been granted, an animal's soul was believed to pass to another animal which would offer itself anew to the hunter at another time. ▲

The seal (phoca hispida) *is found throughout the Arctic, from Alaska to Labrador and Newfoundland. It can remain submerged for more than twenty minutes, but usually reemerges every few minutes to breathe through holes broken in the ice.*

INUIT HUNTERS

Seal hunting.

During the Arctic winter, a long period of time that is barely lit by the sun a few hours a day, the tundra is covered with ice and snow. The men found food by hunting seals on the coast. They usually returned to the same bay they had hunted the previous year. Their most difficult task was locating the ice holes where seals came to breathe at regular intervals. The hunters discovered them with the help of their sled dogs' sense of smell. During the summer, along the Alaskan and Labrador coasts, the Inuit would use *kayaks*, long, narrow, small, canoe-shaped skin boats to hunt walrus. They set forth on the sea that was briefly free of ice in pursuit of sperm whales, narwhals, and porpoises. This last hunt took place in *umiaks*, large thirty foot (10 m) boats made of whalebone and skin. The Inuit traveled in bands of forty to fifty people, including children, typically consisting of about ten to fifteen hunters. They had no chief, but a leader, usually the most experienced, took charge of the hunt. Among the Inuit, the only person who had some degree of community influence was the shaman. A hunter and a father like the other members of the community, he was believed to be able to contact special spirits and to possess the gift of healing.

Most Native people from Alaska to Greenland spoke variations of the same language, Eskimo-Aleut, which branched into two divisions, Yupik and Inuit-Inupiaq, and the other great branch, represented by a single language, Aleut. In spite of very difficult living conditions, the Inuit were a hospitable and happy people and their communal life was filled with warmth and friendship. ▲

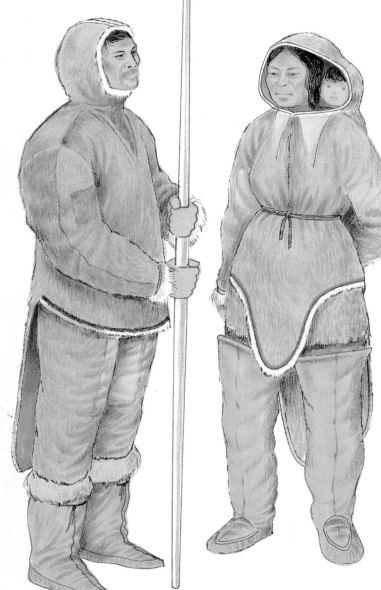

Baffin Inuit in the style of John White, sixteenth century.

Umiak and kayak.

Incising ivory with a bow drill.

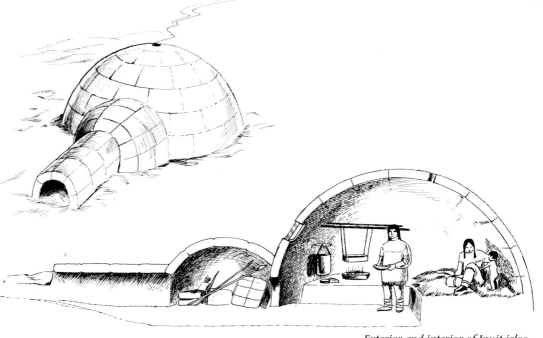

Exterior and interior of Inuit igloo.

Mackenzie Inuit, nineteenth century.

Copper Inuit, nineteenth century.

Igluit Inuit, nineteenth century.

Northern Greenland Inuit, nineteenth century.

INDEX OF NATIVE TRIBES

The boldface numbers refer to illustrations.

IOWA, in the style of George Catlin, 1844.

The author thanks the following organizations for their assistance and support in research.

Musée de l'Homme, Paris
Centre Culturel Américain, Paris
Centre Culturel Canadien, Paris
Centre Culturel Espagnol, Paris
Mojave Country Historical Society, Kingman (Arizona)
Arizona State Museum, Tucson (Arizona)
Historical Association of Southern Florida, Miami (Florida)
Clearwater Historical Society, Orofino (Idaho)
Appaloosa Museum, Moscow (Idaho)
Field Museum, Chicago (Illinois)
Historical Museum, Lansing (Michigan)
Winnebago Area Museum, Winnebago (Minnesota)
State Museum, Jefferson City, Missouri.
Iroquois Indian Museum, Shoharie (New York)
Cherokee Historical Society, Tahlequah (Oklahoma)
Pawnee Bill State Park, Pawnee (Oklahoma)
Provincial Museum, Edmonton (Alberta)
Museum of Northern British Columbia, Prince Rupert (Canada)
Museum of Natural History, Regina (Saskatchewan)
Vancouver Museum, British Columbia (Canada)
The Fine Arts Museum, San Francisco (California)
South Bannock County Historical Center, Lava Spring (Idaho)
Kansas State Historical Society, Topeka (Kansas)
Six Nations Indian Museum, Onchiota (New York)
The Five Civilized Tribes Museum, Muskogee (Oklahoma)
Sioux Indian Museum, Rapid City (South Dakota)
Buffalo Bill Historical Center, Cody (Wyoming)
Algonquian Park, Whitney (Ontario, Canada)
Huron County Museum, Godemich, (Ontario, Canada)
Musée Canadien des Civilisations, Hull (Québec, Canada)
Klamath County Museum, Klamath Falls (Oregon)
University of Maine, Orono (Maine)
Museum of Florida History, Tallahassee (Florida)
University of Oregon, Eugene (Oregon)
Washington State University, Pullman (Washington)

Special thanks to:

Anne Vitard and Daniel Lévine from the Musée de l'Homme in Paris, Carole Caraguel, Éric Bondoux, Maurice Delange, Philippe Grasset, Bernard Gilson, Olivier Legay, and Roland Schmitt.

The author made all maps and illustrations for this work.

Graphics: Nathalie Pecquet, Paris.

Photographic credits:

A. Thomas, Explorer, p. 2 and 32; G. Boutin, Explorer, p. 6 and 11; S. Cordier, Explorer, p. 52; J.-L. Georges, Explorer, p. 60; M. Koene, Explorer, p. 76; R. Baumgartner, Explorer, p. 90; Canadian Embassy, Division of Tourism, p. 84.

First edition for the United States and Canada published 1995 by
Barron's Educational Series, Inc.
English translation © copyright 1995 by Barron's Educational Series, Inc.

© copyright 1993 by Casterman, Tournai, for the original version.

All inquiries should be addressed to:
Barron's Educational Series, Inc.
250 Wireless Boulevard
Hauppauge, New York 11788

Library of Congress Catalog Card No.: 95-13019

International Standard Book No. 0-8120-6515-8

Library of Congress Cataloging-in-Publication Data

Legay, Gilbert.
  [Atlas des Indiens d'Amérique du Nord. English]
  Atlas of Indians of North America / written and illustrated by Gilbert Legay. — 1st ed.
  95 p.   cm. *col ill, col maps*
  Includes index.
  ISBN 0-8120-6515-8
  1. Indians of North America—History—Handbooks, manuals, etc. 2. Indians of North America—Social life and customs—handbooks, manuals, etc.   I. Title.
E77.L574   1995
970.004'97—dc20   *JNF 970.00497 LEGAY*   95-13019
                                                                            CIP

PRINTED IN BELGIUM

567   7150   987654321